Changing the
Racial Attitudes of
Children

PRAEGER SPECIAL STUDIES IN
U.S. ECONOMIC AND SOCIAL DEVELOPMENT

Changing the Racial Attitudes of Children

THE EFFECTS OF AN ACTIVITY GROUP PROGRAM IN NEW YORK CITY SCHOOLS

Julius Trubowitz

FREDERICK A. PRAEGER, Publishers
New York · Washington · London

The purpose of the Praeger Special Studies is to make specialized research monogrphs in U.S. and international economics and politics available to the academic, business, and government communities. For further information, write to the Special Projects Division, Frederick A. Praeger, Publishers, 111 Fourth Avenue, New York, N.Y. 10003.

FREDERICK A. PRAEGER, PUBLISHERS
111 Fourth Avenue, New York, N.Y. 10003, U.S.A.
5, Cromwell Place, London S.W.7, England

Published in the United States of America in 1969
by Frederick A. Praeger, Inc., Publishers

Library of Congress Catalog Card Number: 71-94250

Printed in the United States of America

TO CAROLE

PREFACE

The purpose of this book is to describe and evaluate an experiment to overcome the fear and misunderstanding between races. The aim of the experiment was to change the racial attitudes of Negro and white children. The study tested the effectiveness of interracial contact in certain school activities in inducing positive changes in the racial attitudes of children from selected elementary schools in New York City.

In the past much attention has been given to the success of interracial contact as a method to induce changes in racial attitudes. Interracial contact has been studied in the military, summer camps, colleges, labor unions, and housing projects. Although a number of studies have found positive attitude changes, in some cases attitudes have remained the same or become more negative.

The failure of interracial contact to induce positive attitude change has led to more careful analysis of the conditions of contact. Mere physical presence of members of different races in a common situation has come to be recognized as insufficient to induce positive change of attitude. Research has shown that positive change is more likely to occur in an interracial contact situation that: (1) compels contact among the participants; (2) enables the participants to focus on concrete tasks requiring common effort; (3) provides opportunity for the individuals to interact on a personal basis; (4) places individuals in positions of social equality; and (5) establishes a social norm of friendly interracial relations.

The experiment described in this book focused on six aspects of the interracial contact situation. The influence on attitude change of the following aspects of interracial contact in a school activity group program are evaluated: (1) satisfaction with interracial contact; (2) relative status of the participants; (3) social norm toward contact of one group with another; (4) attitude toward the general activity of interracial contact; (5) perception of the skill of teachers and discussion leaders; and (6) previous attitudes toward classmates and teacher.

CONTENTS

		Page
PREFACE		vii
LIST OF TABLES		xv

Chapter

1	INTRODUCTION	3
	Background	3
	Organization of Interracial Contact Program	4
	Experimental Design	6
	Notes	7
2	THE PROBLEM	8
	Community Interracial Problem	8
	Hypotheses Investigated	8
	Definition of Terms	10
	Limitations of Study	11
3	THEORETICAL FOUNDATIONS AND RELATED LITERATURE	12
	Attitudes of White and Negro People Toward One Another	12
	Attitudes of White People Toward Negro People	12
	Attitudes of Negro People Toward White People	14
	Studies in the Change of Attitudes of White and Negro People Toward One Another Through Interracial Contact	15
	Change in the Attitudes of White People Toward Negro People	15
	Change in the Attitudes of Negro People Toward White People	19
	Summary	20
	Notes	21

4   THE ORGANIZATION OF THE ACTIVITY GROUP
      PROGRAM   24

      Selection and Involvement of School
        Personnel   24
        Selection of Schools   24
        Description of Schools   25
        Liaison with Schools   25
        Involvement of Teachers   26
        Involvement of Discussion Leaders   27
        Selection of Pupils   29
        Introduction of the Program to
          Pupils   29
        Involvement of Parents   30
      Selection and Involvement of Trip Site
        Personnel   30
        Factors in the Selection of Trip
          Sites   .   30
        Liaison with Trip Sites   31
      Description of Experimental Procedure   32
        Experimental Procedure   32
        Selection of Instruments   36
        Description of Subjects   36
      Summary   40
      Notes   43

5   PROCEDURES USED IN COLLECTING DATA   44

      The Attitude Scale   44
      The Social Distance Scale   44
      The Projective Picture Test   45
      Supplementary Tests   45
        My Teacher   46
        Classroom Life   46
        How This Class Thinks   46
      Rating Sheets   46
        The Trip Rating Sheet   47
        The Teacher-Discussion Leader
          Rating Sheet   47
      Observational Material   47
      Parent Reaction   47
      Notes   47

6   BEHAVIOR DURING THE ACTIVITY GROUP
      PROGRAM   49

      Pupil Behavior   49
        Joint-Joint Classes (Fourth Grade)   49
        Joint-Joint Classes (Fifth Grade)   51

        Joint-Separate Classes (Fourth
          Grade)   55
        Joint-Separate Classes (Fifth
          Grade)   57
        Separate-Joint Classes (Fourth
          Grade)   60
        Separate-Joint Classes (Fifth
          Grade)   62
        Separate-Separate Classes (Fourth
          Grade)   63
        Separate-Separate Classes (Fifth
          Grade)   64
      Teacher Behavior   65
        Joint-Joint Teachers (Fourth Grade)   65
        Joint-Joint Teachers (Fifth Grade)   66
        Joint-Separate Teachers (Fourth
          Grade)   68
        Joint-Separate Teachers (Fifth
          Grade)   69
        Separate-Joint Teachers (Fourth
          Grade)   70
        Separate-Joint Teachers (Fifth
          Grade)   71
        Separate-Separate Teachers (Fourth
          Grade)   71
        Separate-Separate Teachers (Fifth
          Grade)   73
      Parent Behavior   73
        Report of Principal of School B
        (White Pupils)   73
        Report of Trip Observers   74
        Report of Test Administrator   74

  7   INITIAL TESTING   75

      The Attitude Scale   75
      The Social Distance Scale   76
      The Projective Picture Test   76
      Correlations of the Pre-Scores of the
        Attitude Measures with Reading and Age   77
      Intercorrelations of the Pre-Scores of
        the Attitude Measures   77

  8   CHANGE RESULTS   78

      The Attitude Scale   78
      The Social Distance Scale   79
      The Projective Picture Test   79

Chapter   Page

      Correlations of the Change Scores of
      the Attitude Measures with Reading
      and Age   80
      Intercorrelations of the Change Scores
      of the Attitude Measures   81
      Test of Hypotheses   81
         Interracial Contact vs. No Contact   81
         Interracial Field Trip Contact vs.
         Interracial Discussion Contact   86
         Summation of Interracial Contact
         vs. Interracial Trip or Interracial
         Discussion Contact   89
         Further Analysis of Findings   94
      Summary of Findings   97

9   SUPPLEMENTARY RESULTS   98

      Partner Relationship   99
         Pupil Perception of Partner   99
         Pupil Evaluations of Own Ideas and
         Partner's Ideas   99
      Trip Properties   102
         Pupil Perception of Trip Experience   102
         Pupil Perception of Teacher   104
         Pupil Perception of Discussion
         Leader   104
         Ratings of Teacher Behavior   107
      Characteristics of Classroom Experience   109
         Pupil Perception of Teacher   109
         Pupil Perception of Classroom Life   109
         Pupil Perception of Class Attitudes   113
      Summary   117

10 SUMMARY AND CONCLUSIONS   121

      Factors Affecting Racial Attitudes   121
         Race   121
         Sex   122
         Age   122
         Reading Ability   123
      Effects of Interracial Contact   123
      Influence of Conditions of Interracial
      Contact   125
         Acquaintance Potential   125
         Relative Status of the Participants   126
         Social Norm Toward Interracial
         Contact   127
         Attitude Toward the Trip Experience   127

Attitude Toward Skill of Authority
    Figures   128
Attitude Toward Own Teacher and
    Classmates   128
  Areas for Future Research   129
  Summary of Experiment   130
    Background   130
    Problem   130
    Focus of Study   131
    Experimental Procedure   131
    Hypotheses   131
    Procedures in Collecting Data   132
    Findings   132
  Notes   132

11 IMPLICATIONS FOR INTERRACIAL CONTACT
    THEORY AND EDUCATIONAL PRACTICE   134

    Notes   139

APPENDIXES

A MEANS, STANDARD DEVIATIONS, TESTS OF
   SIGNIFICANCE, AND GRADE EQUIVALENTS FOR
   READING SCORES OF NEGRO AND WHITE
   SUBJECTS   143

B MEANS, STANDARD DEVIATIONS, AND TESTS
   OF SIGNIFICANCE FOR AGES OF NEGRO AND
   WHITE SUBJECTS   151

C THE ATTITUDE SCALE, THE SOCIAL DISTANCE
   SCALE, THE PROJECTIVE PICTURE TEST,
   SUPPLEMENTARY TESTS, AND RATING SHEETS   157

   Notes   180

D RESULTS OF INITIAL TESTING OF ATTITUDE
   MEASURES: MEANS, STANDARD DEVIATIONS,
   SIGNIFICANCE TESTS OF RACIAL DIFFERENCES,
   TREATMENT GROUP DIFFERENCES, BOY-GIRL
   DIFFERENCES   181

E PRODUCT-MOMENT CORRELATION COEFFICIENTS   197

F MEANS AND STANDARD DEVIATIONS OF PRE-,
   POST-, AND CHANGE SCORES OF THE ATTITUDE
   MEASURES   203

Appendixes   Page

   G   SIGNIFICANCE TESTS OF RACIAL DIFFERENCES
       IN CHANGE SCORES   211

   H   RELATIONSHIPS BETWEEN ITEMS OF TRIP RATING
       SHEETS I AND II AND ATTITUDE SCALE CHANGE
       SCORES   215

BIBLIOGRAPHY   225

ABOUT THE AUTHOR

LIST OF TABLES

Tables   Page

1 Experimental Procedure Used for Fourth
    and Fifth Grades from Schools A and B   33

2 Fourth- and Fifth-Grade Class Assignments
    to Experimental Treatments   34

3 Pupils Eliminated from Study   37

4 Pupils in Activity Group Program by Grade,
    Sex, and School   38

5 Intercorrelations of Reading Scores and
    Age of Fourth- and Fifth-Grade Negro
    and White Experimental Subjects   39

6 Scheffé's Multiple Comparisons Test of
    Hypothesis 1 for Fourth-Grade Negro
    Pupils' Attitude Change Measures   82

7 Scheffé's Multiple Comparisons Test of
    Hypothesis 1 for Fourth-Grade White
    Pupils' Attitude Change Measures   83

8 Scheffé's Multiple Comparisons Test of
    Hypothesis 1 for Fifth-Grade Negro
    Pupils' Attitude Change Measures   84

9 Scheffé's Multiple Comparisons Test of
    Hypothesis 1 for Fifth-Grade White
    Pupils' Attitude Change Measures   85

10 Scheffé's Multiple Comparisons Test of
    Hypothesis 2 for Fourth-Grade Negro
    Pupils' Attitude Change Measures   87

11 Scheffé's Multiple Comparisons Test of
    Hypothesis 2 for Fourth-Grade White
    Pupils' Attitude Change Measures   87

12 Scheffé's Multiple Comparisons Test of
    Hypothesis 2 for Fifth-Grade Negro
    Pupils' Attitude Change Measures   88

13   Scheffé's Multiple Comparisons Test of
     Hypothesis 2 for Fifth-Grade White
     Pupils' Attitude Change Measures   88

14   Scheffé's Multiple Comparisons Test of
     Hypothesis 3 for Fourth-Grade Negro
     Pupils' Attitude Change Measures   90

15   Scheffé's Multiple Comparisons Test of
     Hypothesis 3 for Fourth-Grade White
     Pupils' Attitude Change Measures   91

16   Scheffé's Multiple Comparisons Test of
     Hypothesis 3 for Fifth-Grade Negro
     Pupils' Attitude Change Measures   92

17   Scheffé's Multiple Comparisons Test of
     Hypothesis 3 for Fifth-Grade White
     Pupils' Attitude Change Measures   93

18   Multiple Analysis of Covariance of Attitude
     Scale Post-Scores with Word Knowledge and
     Attitude Scale Pre-Scores as Covariates
     for Fourth- and Fifth-Grade Negro and
     White Pupils   95

19   Attitude Scale Post- and Adjusted Post-
     Means According to Treatment Groups of
     Fourth- and Fifth-Grade Negro and White
     Pupils   96

20   Relationship Between Item 2 of Trip Rating
     Sheets I and II and Attitude Scale
     Change Scores   100

21   Relationship Between Item 3 of Trip Rating
     Sheets I and II and Attitude Scale
     Change Scores   101

22   Relationship Between Item 1 of Trip Rating
     Sheets I and II and Attitude Scale
     Change Scores   103

23   Relationship Between Item 1 of Teacher-
     Discussion Leader Rating Sheet and
     Attitude Scale Change Scores   105

24   Relationship Between Item 2 of Teacher-
     Discussion Leader Rating Sheet and
     Attitude Scale Change Scores   106

Tables   Page

25 Relationship Between Judges' Ratings of
    Teacher Behavior and Attitude Scale
    Change Scores   108

26 Relationship Between Item 8 of My Teacher
    and Attitude Scale Change Scores   110

27 Relationship Between Item 9 of My Teacher
    and Attitude Scale Change Scores   111

28 Relationship Between Item 10 of My Teacher
    and Attitude Scale Change Scores   112

29 Relationship Between Item A of Classroom
    Life and Attitude Scale Change Scores   114

30 Relationship Between Item D of Classroom
    Life and Attitude Scale Change Scores   115

31 Relationship Between Item F of Classroom
    Life and Attitude Scale Change Scores   116

32 Relationship Between Item 4 of How This
    Class Thinks and Attitude Scale Change
    Scores   118

33 Relationship Between Item 5 of How This
    Class Thinks and Attitude Scale Change
    Scores   119

TABLES IN THE APPENDIX

1   Means and Standard Deviations of Reading
    Raw Scores of Fourth-Grade Negro and
    White Pupils by Experimental Treatment
    Groups   145

2   Scheffé's Multiple Comparisons Test of
    Word Knowledge and Reading for Fourth-
    Grade Negro and White Pupils   146

3   Means of Reading Scores in Grade Equiva-
    lents of Fourth-Grade Negro and White
    Pupils by Experimental Treatment Groups   147

4   Means and Standard Deviations of Reading
    Raw Scores of Fifth-Grade Negro and
    White Pupils by Experimental Treatment
    Groups   148

Tables   Page

5   Scheffé's Multiple Comparisons Test of Word Knowledge and Reading for Fifth-Grade Negro and White Pupils   149

6   Means of Reading Scores in Grade Equivalents of Fifth-Grade Negro and White Pupils by Experimental Treatment Groups   150

7   Means and Standard Deviations of Ages in Months of Fourth-Grade Negro and White Pupils by Experimental Treatment Groups   153

8   Scheffé's Multiple Comparisons Test of Age for Fourth-Grade Negro and White Pupils   154

9   Means and Standard Deviations of Ages in Months of Fifth-Grade Negro and White Pupils by Experimental Treatment Groups   155

10   Scheffé's Multiple Comparisons Test of Age for Fifth-Grade Negro and White Pupils   156

11   Means and Standard Deviations of Pre-Scores of the Attitude Scale for Treatment Groups of Negro and White Fourth-Grade Pupils   183

12   Means and Standard Deviations of Pre-Scores of the Social Distance Scale for Treatment Groups of Negro and White Fourth-Grade Pupils   183

13   Means and Standard Deviations of Pre-Scores of the Projective Picture Test for Treatment Groups of Negro and White Fourth-Grade Pupils   184

14   Significance Tests of Racial Differences in Pre-Test Scores of Fourth-Grade Pupils   184

15   Scheffé's Multiple Comparisons Test of Pre-Scores for Fourth-Grade Negro Pupils on the Attitude Measures   185

16   Scheffé's Multiple Comparisons Test of
       Pre-Scores for Fourth-Grade White
       Pupils on the Attitude Measures   186

17   Means, Standard Deviations, and Scheffé's
       Tests of Differences Between Fourth-
       Grade Boys and Girls on the Pre-Test of
       the Attitude Scale   187

18   Means, Standard Deviations, and Scheffé's
       Tests of Differences Between Fourth-
       Grade Boys and Girls on the Pre-Test of
       the Social Distance Scale   188

19   Means, Standard Deviations, and Scheffé's
       Tests of Differences Between Fourth-
       Grade Boys and Girls on the Pre-Test of
       the Projective Picture Test   189

20   Means and Standard Deviations of Pre-Scores
       of the Attitude Scale for Treatment
       Groups of Negro and White Fifth-Grade
        Pupils   190

21   Means and Standard Deviations of Pre-Scores
       of the Social Distance Scale for Treat-
       ment Groups of Negro and White Fifth-
       Grade Pupils   190

22   Means and Standard Deviations of Pre-Scores
       of the Projective Picture Test for
       Treatment Groups of Negro and White
       Fifth-Grade Pupils   191

23   Significance Tests of Racial Differences
       in Pre-Test Scores of Fifth-Grade Pupils   191

24   Scheffé's Multiple Comparisons Test of
       Pre-Scores for Fifth-Grade Negro Pupils
       on the Attitude Measures   192

25   Scheffé's Multiple Comparisons Test of
       Pre-Scores for Fifth-Grade White Pupils
       on the Attitude Measures   193

26   Means, Standard Deviations, and Scheffé's
       Tests of Differences Between Fifth-
       Grade Boys and Girls on the Pre-Test of
       the Attitude Scale   194

Tables   Page

27 Means, Standard Deviations, and Scheffé's
    Tests of Differences Between Fifth-
    Grade Boys and Girls on the Pre-Test of
    the Social Distance Scale   195

28 Means, Standard Deviations, and Scheffé's
    Tests of Differences Between Fifth-
    Grade Boys and Girls on the Pre-Test of
    the Projective Picture Test   196

29 Product-Moment Correlation Coefficients
    Between Pre-Test Scores of the Attitude
    Measures and Reading Scores and Ages for
    Negro and White Fourth- and Fifth-Grade
    Pupils   199

30 Intercorrelations of Pre-Scores of the
    Attitude Scale, the Social Distance
    Scale, and the Projective Picture Test
    for Fourth- and Fifth-Grade Negro and
    White Pupils   200

31 Product-Moment Correlation Coefficients
    Between Change Scores of the Attitude
    Measures and Reading Scores and Ages
    for Negro and White Fourth- and Fifth-
    Grade Pupils   201

32 Intercorrelations of Change Scores of the
    Attitude Scale, the Social Distance
    Scale, and the Projective Picture Test
    for Fourth- and Fifth-Grade Negro and
    White Pupils   202

33 Means and Standard Deviations of Pre-,
    Post-, and Change Scores of the Attitude
    Scale for Treatment Groups of Negro and
    White Fourth-Grade Pupils   205

34 Means and Standard Deviations of Pre-,
    Post-, and Change Scores of the Social
    Distance Scale for Treatment Groups of
    Negro and White Fourth-Grade Pupils   206

35 Means and Standard Deviations of Pre-,
    Post-, and Change Scores of the Projective
    Picture Test for Treatment Groups of
    Negro and White Fourth-Grade Pupils   207

36 Means and Standard Deviations of Pre-,
    Post-, and Change Scores of the Attitude
    Scale for Treatment Groups of Negro and
    White Fifth-Grade Pupils   208

37 Means and Standard Deviations of Pre-,
    Post-, and Change Scores of the Social
    Distance Scale for Treatment Groups of
    Negro and White Fifth-Grade Pupils   209

38 Means and Standard Deviations of Pre-,
    Post-, and Change Scores of the Projective
    Picture Test for Treatment Groups of
    Negro and White Fifth-Grade Pupils   210

39 Significance Tests of Racial Differences
    in Change Scores of Fourth-Grade Pupils   213

40 Significance Tests of Racial Differences
    in Change Scores of Fifth-Grade Pupils   213

41 Relationship Between Item 1 of Trip Rating
    Sheet I and Attitude Scale Change
    Scores   217

42 Relationship Between Item 1 of Trip Rating
    Sheet II and Attitude Scale Change
    Scores   218

43 Relationship Between Item 2 of Trip Rating
    Sheet I and Attitude Scale Change Scores   219

44 Relationship Between Item 2 of Trip Rating
    Sheet II and Attitude Scale Change
    Scores   220

45 Relationship Between Item 3 of Trip Rating
    Sheet I and Attitude Scale Change Scores   221

46 Relationship Between Item 3 of Trip Rating
    Sheet II and Attitude Scale Change
    Scores   222

Changing the
Racial Attitudes of
Children

CHAPTER **1** INTRODUCTION

BACKGROUND

The improvement of Negro and white relationships is one of the most urgent problems confronting schools today. It concerns parent, teacher, administrator, and researcher. John H. Fischer stated, "Virtually every innovation in American schools during the coming decade will be influenced by . . . the growing effort to improve relations between the races."[1]

The racially segregated school represents an obstacle to achieving positive relations between the races. Segregation plays a crucial role in determining the developing attitudes of Negro and white children toward themselves and the world about them. The Supreme Court decision of 1954 stated: "To separate them [Negroes] from others of similar age and qualifications solely because of their race generates a feeling of inferiority as to their status in the community that may affect their hearts and minds in a way unlikely ever to be undone."

Various school integration programs have been proposed and implemented to improve racial attitudes. Schools have been paired to achieve better racial balance. Negro and white children in particular grades have been assigned to one school and those in the remaining grades have been assigned to the other school. Central schools have been established whereby one school building became a central facility for several grades servicing an entire school district. Particular segregated schools have been closed with the students dispersed among remaining schools. Open enrollment plans have permitted a pupil to attend an under-utilized school outside of the attendance zone in which his residence is located. Bussing programs have sought to relieve racial imbalance by transporting Negro children from their normal attendance areas to predominantly white schools in other areas.

Other plans for eliminating school segregation have been the strategic location of new school sites to assure racial balance, adjustment of attendance area boundaries in large school systems, and the placement of Negro pupils from majority-Negro central city schools in neighboring suburban school systems.

In the large urban centers, however, these programs have produced little progress in achieving racial integration in the schools. Fischer, reviewing the progress of school desegregation in big cities, has written:

> Twelve years of effort, some ingeniously pro forma and some laboriously genuine, have proved that desegregating schools . . . is much more difficult than it first appeared. Despite some initial success and a few stable solutions, the consequences, for the most part, have proved disappointing. Steady increases in urban Negro population, continuing shifts in the racial character of neighborhoods, actual or supposed decline in student achievement, unhappiness over cultural differences and unpleasant personal relations have combined to produce new problems faster than old ones could be solved.[2]

An interest in the influence of these factors in interracial relations led the investigator to develop this exploratory field study. It is an attempt to induce racial attitude change among Negro and white children. The programs of two racially segregated schools were experimentally manipulated to bring about interracial contact in an activity group program.

ORGANIZATION OF INTERRACIAL
CONTACT PROGRAM

The interracial contact was organized in a school activity group program of educational trips. In establishing the program the investigator dealt with a number of problems in each of the following areas:

Area 1.   The selection of schools:

      a.   Which schools should be selected?

      b.   What racial composition should exist in the schools?

      c.   How should schools be contacted?

      d.   What support would be required of school administrators?

Area 2.   The involvement of teachers:

      a.   Which teachers should be involved?

      b.   What training should be given the teachers in preparation for the field project?

Area 3.   The selection of discussion leaders:

      a.   How many discussion leaders should be selected?

      b.   What background experience should they have?

      c.   What training should be given the discussion leaders in preparation for the field project?

Area 4.   The selection of pupils:

      a.   What grade levels should be selected for the field project?

      b.   What preparation should pupils receive?

Area 5.   The selection of educational sites:

      a.   Which sites should be selected?

      b.   What type of experience should they offer?

      c.   What physical facilities were required?

      d.   How should trip sites be contacted?

e. What support would be required of trip site officials?

Area 6. The involvement of parents:

a. How much participation should parents have in the field project?

b. What functions could parents carry out?

Area 7. The selection of instruments for measuring the effects of the field experience:

a. What instruments were appropriate for children?

b. What instruments could be read, understood, and responded to appropriately by children?

c. What instruments maintained a high interest level for children and also offered a variety of approaches?

In the process of selection, the investigator interviewed and evaluated school and trip site personnel for suitability. Discussion and role-playing methods were used to prepare and train personnel for participation in the program.

EXPERIMENTAL DESIGN

The Activity Group Program consists of three full-day educational trips. Each trip is divided into two phases. The first, designated the Trip Activity, includes arriving at the trip site, assigning of pupil partners, looking at exhibits and films, listening to talks, and having lunch together. The pupils are instructed to accompany their assigned partners during every aspect of the Trip Activity. There are no restrictions on pupil conversations.

After lunch, in private areas of the respective sites, the second phase begins. This is designated the Discussion Activity and is led by the discussion leader. It consists both of discussions about the trip among the partners and reports to the group as a whole. Thereafter the pupils return to their schools.

   Participants in the program include four fourth-
grade classes and four fifth-grade classes from two
New York City schools, one predominantly Negro, the
other predominantly white. By controlling the assigning of pupil partners, it is possible to vary
the degree of interracial contact during the trips.
Thus some classes experience interracial contact
during both the Trip and Discussion Activities, some
experience interracial contact only during one of
the activities, and the remainder are not exposed to
interracial contact at all. In all cases the partners are of the same grade level and sex.

   Three attitude tests are used to measure the
racial attitudes of the pupils in the study: the
Attitude Scale, the Social Distance Scale, and the
Projective Picture Test. Two rating sheets--Trip
Rating Sheet and Discussion-Leader Rating Sheet--are
devised to determine the pupils' perceptions of the
trip experiences. Discussion leaders and teachers
gather observational material regarding teacher and
pupil trip behavior. A number of supplementary
tests--My Teacher, Classroom Life, and How This
Class Thinks--are also used to gain the pupils' perceptions of life in their classes.

                         NOTES

   1. John H. Fischer, "Innovation and Two Currents of Change," Phi Delta Kappan, XLVI, (1964),
151.

   2. John H. Fischer, "The School Park," in
United States Commission on Civil Rights, ed.,
Racial Isolation in the Public Schools, Vol. 2,
Appendices. (Washington, D.C.: U.S. Government
Printing Office, 1967) pp. 253-54.

CHAPTER **2** THE PROBLEM

COMMUNITY INTERRACIAL PROBLEM

In our multiracial culture it can be assumed that racial attitudes are an important part of every child's psychological development. Previous studies provide evidence that racial attitudes may be unfriendly and derogatory, and that under certain conditions it is possible to develop more positive attitudes through interracial contact.

The main problem of this study was to evaluate the effectiveness of participation in an interracial activity group program in inducing positive change in the racial attitudes of Negro and white fourth- and fifth-grade children. In the Activity Group Program two types of interracial contact--a field trip and a discussion experience--were experimentally manipulated so that the cumulative and separate effects of the two experiences could be evaluated.

The analysis of the interracial activity group program as a useful tool for inducing positive attitude change is based on Cook's three-dimensional description of the nature of the interracial contact experience. These are (1) acquaintance potential; (2) relative status of the participants in the two ethnic groups; and (3) nature of the social norm toward contact of one ethnic group with another.

As a means of studying the effects of the experimental manipulation, data were gathered through the use of attitude measures, rating sheets, supplementary classroom tests, and observational techniques. These will be described in Chapter 5.

HYPOTHESES INVESTIGATED

Hypothesis 1. It was predicted that greater positive changes in racial attitudes would be found in pupils

8

and sexes, and (2) intercorrelations among age, reading ability, and racial attitudes.

DEFINITION OF TERMS

Interracial Attitude or Racial Attitude. Herein, interracial attitude or racial attitude includes the perceptions, thoughts, and emotions that a Negro pupil holds toward a white pupil and that a white pupil holds toward a Negro pupil.

Interracial Trip Activity (Joint Trip). A part of the school program with Negro and white pupils jointly visiting a museum, library, or other site of educational value.

Interracial Discussion Activity (Joint Discussion). A part of the school program with Negro and white pupils jointly sharing their reactions to the trip.

Separate Trip Activity (Separate Trip). A part of the school program with Negro and white pupils separately visiting a museum, library, or other site of educational value.

Separate Discussion Activity (Separate Discussion). A part of the school program with Negro and white pupils separately sharing their reactions to the trip.

Discussion Leader. A skilled adult who leads the Discussion Activity following each trip.*

Segregated School. A school where at least 85 percent of the pupils are from one racial group.

Trip Observer. An adult who observes teacher and pupil behavior throughout the Trip Activity.

Teacher. The regular classroom teacher who accompanies his class throughout the Trip Activity and serves as observer during the Discussion Activity.

Partners. The paired pupils assigned to each other during the Trip and Discussion Activities.

------

*The investigator and two other individuals served as Discussion Leaders during the study.

who experienced interracial contact in the Activity
Group Program than in those who experienced no such
interracial contact.

Hypothesis 1 was based on the accumulated evidence that interracial contact can be effective in
inducing a positive attitude change.

Hypothesis 2. It was predicted that among participants in the program greater positive changes in
racial attitudes would be found in pupils who experienced interracial discussion contact.

Hypothesis 2 developed from the differences in
the characteristics of the two activities--Trip
Activity and Discussion Activity. The Trip Activity
was organized so that pupils could develop more personal relationships. The pupils walked together,
conversed together, viewed museum exhibits together,
and had lunch together. These activities occurred
in an informal atmosphere which minimized differences
in academic ability. Since the Trip Activity occupied the greater part of the museum experience,
pupils had more time to interact. The Discussion
Activity, on the other hand, presented a more limited opportunity for pupils to interact and build
personal relationships. The activity included a discussion in which pupils shared their trip reactions
and came to an agreement with their partners. In
comparison with the Trip Activity, this period was
more structured and more formal.

Hypothesis 3. It was predicted that among participants in the program greater positive changes in
racial attitudes would be found in pupils who experienced both interracial trip contact and discussion
contact than in those who experienced only the one
or the other.

Hypothesis 3 was based on the characteristics
of the combined experiences compared to either one
The combined experience of Trip and Discussion
Activities was of longer duration and offered grea
opportunities for the participants to build perso
relationships.

The hypotheses were tested separately for ｐ
in the fourth and fifth grades.

The following sub-problems were studied:
racial attitude differences between races, grａ

and sexes, and (2) intercorrelations among age, reading ability, and racial attitudes.

DEFINITION OF TERMS

Interracial Attitude or Racial Attitude. Herein, interracial attitude or racial attitude includes the perceptions, thoughts, and emotions that a Negro pupil holds toward a white pupil and that a white pupil holds toward a Negro pupil.

Interracial Trip Activity (Joint Trip). A part of the school program with Negro and white pupils jointly visiting a museum, library, or other site of educational value.

Interracial Discussion Activity (Joint Discussion). A part of the school program with Negro and white pupils jointly sharing their reactions to the trip.

Separate Trip Activity (Separate Trip). A part of the school program with Negro and white pupils separately visiting a museum, library, or other site of educational value.

Separate Discussion Activity (Separate Discussion). A part of the school program with Negro and white pupils separately sharing their reactions to the trip.

Discussion Leader. A skilled adult who leads the Discussion Activity following each trip.*

Segregated School. A school where at least 85 percent of the pupils are from one racial group.

Trip Observer. An adult who observes teacher and pupil behavior throughout the Trip Activity.

Teacher. The regular classroom teacher who accompanies his class throughout the Trip Activity and serves as observer during the Discussion Activity.

Partners. The paired pupils assigned to each other during the Trip and Discussion Activities.

---

*The investigator and two other individuals served as Discussion Leaders during the study.

who experienced interracial contact in the Activity
Group Program than in those who experienced no such
interracial contact.

Hypothesis 1 was based on the accumulated evidence that interracial contact can be effective in
inducing a positive attitude change.

Hypothesis 2. It was predicted that among participants in the program greater positive changes in
racial attitudes would be found in pupils who experienced interracial discussion contact.

Hypothesis 2 developed from the differences in
the characteristics of the two activities--Trip
Activity and Discussion Activity. The Trip Activity
was organized so that pupils could develop more personal relationships. The pupils walked together,
conversed together, viewed museum exhibits together,
and had lunch together. These activities occurred
in an informal atmosphere which minimized differences
in academic ability. Since the Trip Activity occupied the greater part of the museum experience,
pupils had more time to interact. The Discussion
Activity, on the other hand, presented a more limited opportunity for pupils to interact and build
personal relationships. The activity included a discussion in which pupils shared their trip reactions
and came to an agreement with their partners. In
comparison with the Trip Activity, this period was
more structured and more formal.

Hypothesis 3. It was predicted that among participants in the program greater positive changes in
racial attitudes would be found in pupils who experienced both interracial trip contact and discussion
contact than in those who experienced only the one
or the other.

Hypothesis 3 was based on the characteristics
of the combined experiences compared to either one.
The combined experience of Trip and Discussion
Activities was of longer duration and offered greater
opportunities for the participants to build personal
relationships.

The hypotheses were tested separately for pupils
in the fourth and fifth grades.

The following sub-problems were studied: (1)
racial attitude differences between races, grades,

Limitations of Study

The study was limited to two elementary schools in New York City. One school was a segregated white school in the Bronx. The other was a segregated Negro school in Manhattan. The white pupils represented a lower middle class socioeconomic background and the Negro pupils a lower class background.

The study included only fourth- and fifth-grade pupils. A total of sixteen classes participated: eight fourth-grade and eight fifth-grade.

Sixteen teachers took part in the study. Of this total, only two were Negro.

The activity group program lasted three months and was limited to three full-day educational trips.

CHAPTER **3** THEORETICAL
FOUNDATIONS
AND RELATED
LITERATURE

Background material pertinent to the study is
presented in two sections. One concerns attitudes
of white and Negro people toward one another. The
other deals with changes in these attitudes as the
result of interracial contact.

ATTITUDES OF WHITE AND NEGRO PEOPLE
TOWARD ONE ANOTHER

Attitudes of White People
Toward Negro People

The available research on attitudes of white
people toward Negroes indicates that: (1) white
children show preference for their own race in
friendship choices and general evaluation; (2) white
children tend to have negative attitudes toward
Negroes; and (3) the interracial attitudes of white
people are directly taught or subtly developed early
in childhood.

Joan H. Criswell, in an analysis of the sociometric data of children in racially mixed classes
from kindergarten through eighth grade in several
New York City schools, found that both white and
Negro pupils showed an increasing tendency to prefer
members of their own race as they grew older.[1]
White children surpassed Negro children in self-
preference tendencies at all grade levels and mutual
withdrawal of the two groups became very pronounced
in the fifth grade.

Marian Radke, Jean Sutherland, and Pearl Rosenberg studied Negro and white children aged seven to
thirteen in a low socioeconomic area of Pittsburgh.[2]
When they were shown pictures of Negro and white

12

people, Negro children assigned undesirable characteristics to members of their race, while white
children assigned almost no undesirable characteristics to members of theirs. White children of all
ages expressed strong preferences for their own
racial group. Interracial choice was limited
strictly to the classroom. It was not carried to
the community, where the ratio of Negro people to
white people was the same as in the school.

Radke and Trager tested racial attitudes among
more than 200 Negro and white children from kindergarten through second grade in six Philadelphia
schools.[3] Through interviews and the use of dolls
of different skin color, they found that 89 percent
of the white children preferred a white doll, while
only 57 percent of the Negro children preferred a
Negro doll.

In 1942, Paul L. Boynton and George D. Mayo
used questionnaires to measure attitudes of white
high school students toward Negroes.[4] The biggest
differences between races were found in the area of
social relations. In 1948, the same questionnaire
was administered again. This time racial attitudes
toward the Negro were found to have improved. But
in the area of social proximity, white students were
still found to harbor negative attitudes.[5]

Negative attitudes and distorted perceptions
have been directly taught in some instances, according to Eugene Horowitz and Ruth Horowitz.[6] They cite
a white child in Tennessee who had been taught by
means of a whip to stay away from Negro children. In
general, Eugene Horowitz states later: "Children
come in contact with the prevailing attitude very
early and these attitudes are more or less subtly
taught the children as they grow older? . . ."[7]

Radke and Sutherland found that fifth- through
twelfth-grade children in a small Midwest town, who
had little or no contact with minority groups, held
derogatory attitudes toward--and strong stereotypes
of--a Negro.[8]

Bruno Lasker's early study, based on the observations and autobiographical data of a large adult
group, revealed the influence of family, friends, and
school experiences in developing the seeds of racial
and religious attitudes in early childhood.[9]

The above studies demonstrate how negative racial attitudes become an integral part of the child's overall development.

Attitudes of Negro People
Toward White People

The available research on attitudes of Negro people toward white people indicates that: (1) interracial attitudes of Negro children develop early in childhood; (2) the Negro person has negative feelings toward his own race; and (3) the Negro person tends to attribute more desirable characteristics to white people.

Kenneth Clark and Mamie Clark studied the racial preference of Negro children aged three to seven by using drawings and crayons.[10] The majority of the children, they found, preferred to color the human figures white and yellow. The children described the black or brown colored areas with strong negative feelings, such as "nigger" and "dirty." The same authors found in another study that when faced with certain choices in evaluating brown or white dolls, the majority of 253 Negro children aged three to seven tended to prefer the white doll and to negate the brown doll.[11]

Using the Guilford-Zimmerman Temperament Survey with 240 Negro male and female subjects who were randomly assigned to one of four groups and told to answer the survey as Negro male, Negro female, white male, and white female, James Bayton, Lettie Austin, and Kay Burke found that the Negro subjects viewed white people as higher in general activity, ascendance, stability, and restraint.[12] The authors suggested that, in terms of basic impression, the results were in the same direction as an earlier study by Bayton. In the earlier study, Bayton used the Katz and Braly adjective list to identify the racial stereotypes of 100 Negro college students.

Radke, Sutherland, and Rosenberg found that Negro children in a predominantly Negro school sought friendship in both races.[13] The white children chose friends within their own group at a higher frequency (75 percent), while only 21 percent of the Negro children made friendship choices entirely within their own race. The Negro boys also showed a slight preference for white girls over Negro girls. The same study also found that sixth-grade Negro children

were more hostile toward the white group, but that
they had more "positive" feelings toward their own
race than did younger Negro children. As the Negro
child gets older, he comes into conflict about the
"goodness" of his own group, and shows "increased
antagonism towards the white group." He is unwill-
ing to accept inferior social status because of race.

STUDIES IN THE CHANGE OF ATTITUDES OF WHITE
AND NEGRO PEOPLE TOWARD ONE ANOTHER
THROUGH INTERRACIAL CONTACT

Change in the Attitudes of White
People Toward Negro People

The available research on changes of attitude
of white and Negro people toward one another through
interracial contact indicates that: (1) Negro and
white people who have experienced satisfying interracial contact are more likely to express a preference for further contact; (2) positive change of
attitude is more likely when Negro and white people
have an opportunity to interact on a personal level;
(3) Negro and white people who have contact on an
equal status basis are more likely to have a positive change of attitude; (4) Negro and white people
who view their peers as approving of interracial
contact tend to change positively in an interracial
situation; (5) when authority persons communicate
that friendly association between races is desirable,
positive change of attitude is more likely; and (6)
Negro and white people may experience considerable
conflict in interracial situations. The Negro person tends to be uncertain about his role and may
express hostility. The white person may be aggressive and resist contact.

Stuart W. Cook has analyzed the relationship
between interracial contact and attitude change.14
He presented three dimensions for evaluating the
effectiveness of the contact situation for inducing
positive attitude change. One dimension of the
interracial situation concerned the opportunity it
offered for personal interaction. Some interracial
situations, such as contact with a Negro elevator
operator, may place strict limitations on the areas
of communication. Another interracial situation--
that of living as neighbors--does not impose com-
parable limitations on the basis of communication.
Cook called this dimension--the extent to which an

interracial situation offered the opportunity to get to know one another--acquaintance potential.

A second dimension involved the relative status levels of the participants in an interracial situation. For example, one interracial situation may place Negroes in a menial job while white persons are in supervisory positions; in another work situation, Negroes and whites may be doing the same kinds of jobs.

The third dimension concerned the nature of the social norm toward interracial contact. In some interracial situations, the general expectation of persons in authority and of most of the participants may be that friendly association between members of the two groups is appropriate; in other situations, the general feeling of persons in authority and on the part of at least one of the groups may be that any unnecessary mingling should be avoided.

Various investigations have attempted to demonstrate the positive effects of interracial contact. Morton Deutsch and Mary Collins found that white women in an integrated housing project respected and liked the Negroes in general.[15] The study illustrated how a situation which offered varied opportunities for individuals to interact on a personal level with one another resulted in a change of attitudes. Samples from some of the interviews with white housewives in the housing project illustrated this process. One woman said:

> I started to cry when my husband
> told me we were coming to live here.
> I cried for three weeks. . . . I
> didn't want to come and live here
> where there are so many colored
> people. I didn't want to bring my
> children up with colored children,
> but we had to come; there was no
> place else to go. . . . Well, all
> that's changed. I've really come
> to like it. I see they're just as
> human as we are. They have nice
> apartments, they keep their children
> clean, and they're very friendly.
> I've come to like them a great deal.
> I'm no longer scared of them. . . .
> I'd just as soon live near a colored

> person as a white; it makes no dif-
> ference to me.

Another woman said:

> I thought I was moving into the heart
> of Africa. . . . I had always heard
> things about how they were. . . .
> they were dirty, drink a lot . . .
> were like savages. Living with them
> my ideas have changed altogether.
> They're just people. . . . They're
> not any different.

A third said:

> I was prejudiced when I moved in but
> not any more. . . . I find there is
> no such thing as "my kind". . . . I
> was under the impression that every
> colored man that looked at you wanted
> to rape you or was going to pull out
> a razor . . . I don't feel that way
> any more. . . . I know the people. . . .
> I have been in their homes. . . .
> been to church with them. . . . I
> know they're not dirty. My doctor is
> colored. . . . My dentist is colored.
> He's a surgeon and he's wonderful.

Samuel Stouffer, Shirley Star, and Robin
Williams reported the results of integrating volun-
teer Negro platoons and white platoons during combat
in World War II.[16] Men already in a company that
contained a Negro platoon were most favorable toward
it, whereas men in units where there were no mixed
companies were less favorable. The overwhelming
majority of white officers and men gave approval to
the Negroes' performance in combat. They rated the
Negro soldiers equal to the white soldiers in combat
performance. One white sergeant from North Carolina
commented: "These here are just the same as we are
in combat." A white commander from Tennessee said
of the Negroes: "Good cooperation in combat. They
were treated as soldier to soldier. Now they play
ball, joke, and box together." The study suggested
that the likelihood of a positive change increased
when interracial contact involved individuals who
interacted on an equal status basis.

Radke-Yarrow, Campbell, and Yarrow, in a study of interracial camping experiences, found that the situational structure of the camp brought about conformity to new norms despite the habits, practices, and attitudes of the white children before the experience.[17] The leader or counselor was a critical variable in the camp, since he gave definition to the ambiguity of the situation. His own handling of racial issues played a decisive role in communicating new norms to the white children.

The effect of the social norm was seen in Daniel Wilner, Rosabelle Walkley, and Stuart Cook's study of relationships within biracial public housing projects.[18] The authors found that white housewives who believed that the other white women in the project approved of such association showed much more favorable attitudes toward Negroes than those who believed that the other white women disapproved of such association.

School investigations of interracial contact found that white pupils have shown a positive change of racial attitude. A recent survey of a metropolitan center in the Northeast indicated that white pupils who have not attended class with Negroes were likely to express a preference for segregated classrooms, while those who have been in desegregated classrooms were more likely to prefer desegregated classrooms. Moreover, white students whose interracial education began in the early grades were even more likely to prefer desegregated schools than whites whose first association with Negroes in school was in the upper elementary or secondary grades.[19]

The same survey data suggested that school interracial contact had its greatest impact upon student attitudes and preferences through the mediating influence of friendship with students of the other race. Negro and white students who attended school with each other, but had no friends of the other race, were less likely to prefer desegregated situations than students in desegregated schools who had such friends. Having attended schools with students of the other race and having friends of the other race contributed to preferences for desegration. The effect was strongest for students who had both experiences.

Other investigations of interracial contact have produced results in which the attitudes of white

pupils either remained the same or became more unfavorable. Bonita Valien's report on the process of
desegregation in Cairo, Illinois, noted that the
experience strengthened the negative stereotypes that
the white pupils had of the Negro.[20] The lack of
preparation for the pupils and the resistance to integration in the adult population failed to produce
a social norm supportive of the interracial contact.
Staten Webster reported that white pupils from
racially segregated schools who were placed in an
integrated junior high school were less willing to
accept members of the Negro group after a year of
integration than they had been before integration.[21]
Donald Lombardi and Paul Whitmore reported similar
results.[22]

Change in the Attitudes of Negro
People Toward White People

In the Webster study, the Negro students were
more willing to accept the white children after integration than before.[23] Virginia Axline reported that
Negro children in an interracial play therapy situation showed a positive change of racial attitude.[24]

In a later study, Radke-Yarrow, Campbell, and
Yarrow found that Negro girls in an interracial camp
directed less aggression toward white girls than
toward their Negro peers.[25] They also devalued their
Negro peers but overvalued white girls. At the end
of the two-week period at camp, however, self-
rejection had lessened somewhat and patterns of in-
group isolation had begun to subside. The white
girls resisted integration more than the Negro girls.
This was demonstrated by aggressive behavior toward
Negro girls, preference for white girls on sociometric choices, more favorable descriptions of white
girls than of Negro girls, and by the bestowal of
little attention to the Negro girls in their peer-
appraisals. Negro boys were initially more sensitive
concerning aggression among their peers. But at the
end of the two-week period, the Negro boy "was able
to see and discuss aggression of white peers as well."
The contact had helped to reduce apprehension and
create readier acceptance of interracial contacts.

In a 1962 study in Louisville, Kentucky, students were allowed to choose the high school they
would attend.[26] Most of the Negro students who
chose a majority-white high school previously had
attended desegregated elementary or junior high

schools. Most of the Negroes who chose a segregated Negro school had not. The study concluded: "The inference is strong that Negro high school students prefer biracial education only if they have experienced it before. If a Negro student has not received his formative education in biracial schools, the chances are he will not choose to enter one in his more mature years."

Miriam Goldberg reported that in sociometric ratings of Negro and white children in a newly integrated school, the Negro pupils rated white pupils higher than they did each other, while the white pupils rated each other higher than the Negroes.[27] The results suggested that a condition of unequal status existed in the interracial contact.

The Negro child experiences considerable conflict when placed in contact with whites. As the above studies suggest, he may be cautious in his relationships with white people, and in some instances "hostile."

SUMMARY

The previous research has cited various factors of the interracial contact situation related to positive change of attitude. Opportunity for participants to interact on an informal, personal level has been conducive to positive change of attitude. Equal status relationship between Negro and white has been a contributing factor to positive change. The attitude on the part of authority figures that friendly association between the races is desirable has been supportive of positive change.

The investigator in this study has incorporated these factors into the Activity Group Program. Firstly, the interracial contact in the program—Negro and white partner assignments in an educational trip setting—was designed so that pupils could interact informally on a personal level. There were opportunities for Negro and white children to exchange ideas, to enjoy the activities together, to eat together, and to get to know one another. No restrictions were placed on pupil interaction. Second, the informal, nonacademic atmosphere of the trip setting minimized any status differences in terms of classroom skills. The partner assignments themselves were designed to communicate that each pupil was an equal member. The authority persons in the program--teachers, discussion leaders, and trip site personnel--were instructed to communicate an equal acceptance of pupils of both races. Finally, the authority persons were trained to communicate a social norm which indicated that friendly contact between the Negro and white pupils was appropriate and desirable.

NOTES

1. Joan H. Criswell, "A Sociometric Study of Race Cleavage in the Classroom," Archives of Psychology, LXIII (1939), 1-82.

2. Marian Radke, Jean Sutherland, and Pearl Rosenberg, "Racial Attitudes of Children," Sociometry, XIII (1950), 154-71.

3. Marian Radke and Helen G. Trager, "Children's Perceptions of the Social Roles of Negroes and Whites," Journal of Psychology, XXIX (1950), 3-33.

4. Paul L. Boynton and George D. Mayo, "A Comparison of Certain Attitudinal Responses of White and Negro High School Students," Journal of Negro Education, XI (1942), 487-94.

5. George D. Mayo and John R. Kinzer, "A Comparison of the Racial Attitudes of White and Negro High School Students in 1940 and 1948," Journal of Psychology, XXIX (1950), 397-405.

6. Eugene L. Horowitz and Ruth E. Horowitz, "Development of Social Attitudes in Children," Sociometry, I (1938), 301-38.

7. Eugene L. Horowitz, "Race Attitudes," in Otto Klineberg, ed., Characteristics of the Negro (New York: Harper and Bros., 1944), p. 183.

8. Marian Radke and Jean Sutherland, "Children's Concepts About Minority and Majority American Groups," Journal of Educational Psychology, XL (1949), 449-68.

9. Bruno Lasker, Race Attitudes in Children (New York: Henry Holt and Co., 1929).

10. Kenneth B. Clark and Mamie P. Clark, "Emotional Factors in Racial Identification and Preference in Negro Children," Journal of Negro Education, XIX (1950), 341-50.

11. Kenneth B. Clark and Mamie P. Clark, "Racial Identification and Preference in Negro Children," in Eleanor E. Maccoby, Theodore M. Newcomb, and Eugene L. Hartley, eds., Readings in Social Psychology (New York: Henry Holt and Co., 1958), pp. 602-11.

12. James A. Bayton, Lettie J. Austin, and Kay R. Burke, "Negro Perception of Negro and White Personality Traits," Journal of Personality and Social Psychology, I (1965), 250-53.

13. Radke, Sutherland, and Rosenberg, "Racial Attitudes of Children," loc. cit.

14. Stuart W. Cook, "Desegregation: A Psychological Analysis," The American Psychologist, XII (1957), 1-13.

15. Morton Deutsch and Mary E. Collins, "The Effect of Public Policy in Housing Projects upon Interracial Attitudes," in Eleanor E. Maccoby, Theodore M. Newcomb, and Eugene L. Hartley, eds., Readings in Social Psychology (New York: Henry Holt and Co., 1958), pp. 612-23.

16. Samuel A. Stouffer, Shirley A. Star, and Robin M. Williams, Jr., The American Soldier: Adjustment During Army Life. "Studies in Social Psychology in World War II," Vol. 1. (Princeton, N.J.: Princeton University Press, 1949).

17. Marian Radke-Yarrow, John D. Campbell, and Leon F. Yarrow, "Interpersonal Dynamics in Racial Integration," in Eleanor E. Maccoby, Theodore M. Newcomb, and Eugene L. Hartley, eds., Readings in Social Psychology (New York: Henry Holt and Co., 1958), pp. 623-36.

18. Daniel M. Wilner, Rosabelle P. Walkley, and Stuart W. Cook, Human Relations in Interracial Housing, a Study of the Contact Hypothesis (Minneapolis: University of Minnesota Press, 1955).

19. James S. Coleman et al., "Equality of Educational Opportunity," in United States Commission

on Civil Rights, ed., Racial Isolation in the Public Schools, Vol. 2, Appendices (Washington, D.C.: U.S. Government Printing Office, 1967), pp. 21-47.

20. Bonita Valien, "Community in Chaos, Cairo, Illinois," in Robin M. Williams, Jr., and Margaret W. Ryan, eds., Schools in Transition: Community Experience in Desegregation (Chapel Hill: The University of North Carolina Press, 1954), pp. 80-110.

21. Staten W. Webster, "The Influence of Interracial Contact on Social Acceptance in a Newly Integrated School," Journal of Educational Psychology, LII (1961), 292-96.

22. Donald N. Lombardi, "Factors Affecting Change in Attitudes Toward Negroes Among High School Students," Journal of Negro Education, XXXII (1963), 129-36; and Paul G. Whitmore, Jr., "A Study of Desegregation: Attitude Change and Scale Validation" (unpublished Ph.D. dissertation, University of Tennessee, 1956).

23. Webster, loc. cit.

24. Virginia M. Axline, "Play Therapy and Race Conflict in Young Children," Journal of Abnormal and Social Psychology, XLIII (1948), 300-10.

25. Radke-Yarrow, Campbell, and Yarrow, "Interpersonal Dynamics in Racial Integration, loc. cit.

26. United States Commission on Civil Rights, ed., Civil Rights, U.S.A. Public Schools Southern States (Washington, D.C.: U.S. Government Printing Office, 1962), p. 30.

27. Miriam L. Goldberg, "Factors Affecting Educational Attainment in Depressed Urban Areas," in A. Harry Passow, ed., Education in Depressed Areas (New York: Teachers College, Columbia University, 1963), pp. 68-99.

CHAPTER **4** THE ORGANIZATION
OF THE ACTIVITY
GROUP PROGRAM*

In this chapter important aspects of the Activity Group Program are considered: preparation for the program; the nature of the schools and subjects; and the nature and sequence of the activities in the experimental program.

SELECTION AND INVOLVEMENT
OF SCHOOL PERSONNEL

Selection of Schools

The selection of the two schools to participate in the study was determined by three factors: (1) the interest and cooperation of the principal; (2) the racial composition of the school; and (3) the location of the school.

The investigator interviewed a number of principals to explore the feasibility of their schools participating in the study and to describe the nature and goals of the program. The following areas were explored with the principals: class selection, teacher selection and cooperation, parent reaction, selection of trip sites, transportation, and trip schedules.

Since the principal could influence his school's attitude toward the program, selection of the principal was of particular importance. The investigator eliminated principals who seemed reluctant to give the required commitment. Principals who seemed cautious and hesitant to try new programs were not selected. Principals who seemed motivated mainly

---

*Tables 1-5.

24

by the prestige of involvement in a research program
were considered undesirable. In the two schools
selected, the principals expressed a genuine interest
in the experimentation. They asserted that the program would provide an invaluable experience for the
pupils in their school. They seemed deeply concerned
about the problem of interracial relations and indicated a readiness to meet with any parent to discuss
the program. The principals planned to meet with
participating teachers to emphasize the school's support of the program, the value of the program to the
pupils, and its significance in dealing with an immediate social problem.

The schools fulfilled the requirements of racial
composition and location. More than a majority of
the pupils in each school (85 percent) represented a
different racial group. Both schools were a part of
the same urban system, facilitating a coordinated
program.

Description of Schools

The schools referred to in this report are
designated as School A and School B. School A is
located in the East Harlem section of Manhattan.
The school population is predominantly Negro with
no white children in attendance. The neighborhood
is mainly Negro lower class with a smaller percentage of Puerto Ricans. School B is in the Pelham
Parkway section of the Bronx. The school population
is predominantly white with a small percentage of
Negro and Puerto Rican children. The neighborhood
is mainly white lower middle class. School B serv-
ices small areas of low socioeconomic families living
on the outskirts of the school district.

The classes in each school are grouped according
to reading achievement level. The design of the
study required the participation of four classes on
each of two grade levels. Thus classes of different
reading levels were used since they were the only
ones available. Since the pupil population and class
sizes in the two schools were different, the numbers
in the classes participating in the study were different.

Liaison with Schools

After the principals of the schools agreed to
participate in the program, all arrangements,

schedules, meetings, and problems were handled
through the assistant principals in the respective
schools. They helped to select the trip sites and
assisted in scheduling meetings with the participating teachers. The investigator and the assistant
principals organized the testing and trip schedules
so that they would not conflict with other school
activities. The assistant principals helped in ob-
taining transportation for the classes to the trip
sites and back to the schools. They kept the investigator informed of teacher absences. Throughout
the Activity Group Program, the assistant principals
were invaluable contacts as they were readily available and extremely cooperative.

Involvement of Teachers

    The selection of teachers was determined by the
design of the study and the recommendations of the
principals. Since fourth- and fifth-grade classes
were included in the study, only teachers on these
grade levels were involved. In discussions with
the principals, the investigator indicated that the
interracial attitudes of participating teachers would
be a significant influence on pupil reaction. Tests
or questionnaires to assess interracial attitudes of
teachers were considered a possible source of teacher
resentment and impractical to administer. Therefore,
teacher selection was based on the knowledge and
evaluation of the principals. The investigator instructed the principals to judge teachers according
to the following criteria: (1) emotional maturity;
(2) willingness to participate in new programs; and
(3) unprejudiced personality.

    The investigator met with the participating
teachers prior to the Activity Group Program to gain
their cooperation and to orient them to the procedures and goals of the program. During a series
of informal meetings, the teachers gave their reactions to an overview of the program and a number of
questions were discussed.

    The various aspects of the teachers' role in
the study--introducing the program to the pupils,
organizing the classes during the Trip Activity,
and observing pupil behavior during the Discussion
Activity--were presented and analyzed. The investigator discussed the influence of the teachers' own
interracial attitudes on the program. He pointed
out that their behavior would be an important

determinant influencing the reactions of the pupils
to the program. The investigator raised the questions of how the teachers felt about Negro and white
children participating on a trip and attending school
together. The teachers felt it was beneficial for
both Negro and white children and expressed support
for the interracial contact in the program and in
schools. Some concern was expressed regarding the
reactions of the pupils, and the following important
questions were raised: (1) How does a teacher deal
with pupils who are reluctant to join their assigned
partners? and (2) How does a teacher handle a parent
who comes to complain about the interracial aspects
of the program? The investigator organized role-
playing situations depicting these problems and gave
all the teachers an opportunity to participate. Discussions after the role-playing helped to develop
greater skill and understanding in dealing with these
situations.

The investigator gave further emphasis to the
interracial attitudes of the teachers. He designed
a role-playing situation of a group of teachers discussing the interracial program. The role-playing
and a discussion led by the investigator helped
teachers to express their feelings toward interracial
contact and strengthened their positive attitudes
toward the program.

In the discussion concerning the teachers' role
during the program, the investigator emphasized that
an attitude of acceptance of interracial contact and
the expectation of friendly interracial contact were
essential. Further specific problems, such as fric-
tion between partners, were discussed.

Involvement of Discussion Leaders

The Activity Group Program consisted of three
trips for each class and a total of thirty-six Discussion Activities. To effectively carry out the
task of observing pupils during the Trip Activity
and leading the discussions, several discussion
leaders were required. Three discussion leaders
were selected to achieve a reasonable assignment of
tasks. Each class met once with each discussion
leader. In this way the influence of the discussion
leader in the Activity Group Program was controlled
through equal exposure for all pupils.

The investigator interviewed many individuals
in selecting discussion leaders. The following
factors were considered: (1) teaching experience
with the age group participating in the study; (2)
skills in leading discussions; and (3) interest in
the project. All of the selected discussion leaders
had at least three years of teaching experience in
the grade levels used in the study. The investigator
evaluated those selected as having superior verbal
skills, intelligence, sensitivity, and a keen interest
in the program.

The investigator met with the discussion leaders
in a number of informal sessions prior to the Activity Group Program. The investigator provided an overview of the program with emphasis on a presentation
and analysis of the two aspects of the discussion
leaders' role: trip observer and discussion leader.
The discussion leaders gave their reactions and
raised various questions about the program.

The investigator stressed the importance of the
discussion leaders' own interracial attitudes as an
influence during the program. The investigator
raised the questions of how the discussion leaders
felt about Negro and white children participating in
a trip and attending school together. The discussion
leaders felt that it was beneficial for both Negro
and white children, and they expressed support for
the interracial contact in the program and in schools.
The investigator designed a role-playing situation of
a group of adults discussing interracial contact.
The role-playing and a discussion helped the discussion leaders to express their feelings about interracial contact and strengthened their positive
attitudes toward the program.

The investigator raised the issue of racial
stereotyping and how it might influence observational reports. The investigator emphasized the
need for clear, objective standards for observations.
To develop uniform, objective standards for describing behavior, the investigator arranged for discussion leaders to participate in a number of training
exercises in which they observed several sessions
in an interracial playground situation. The discussion leaders recorded their observations separately,
discussed their observations, and agreed on guide-
lines for such behaviors as friendly pupil interaction, aggressive pupil interaction, adult behavior

supportive of interracial contact, and adult behavior
inhibiting interracial contact.

The discussion leaders were each given an opportunity to role-play a Discussion Activity situation.
After the role-playing, the investigator led discussions to further develop skill and understanding in
dealing with the Discussion Activity. The investigator emphasized that a pleasant, calm approach was
essential. Further specific problems, such as fric-
tion between partners and withdrawal from partners,
were discussed.

The observations, role-playing, and discussions
helped discussion leaders to clarify their roles,
to develop uniform standards of behavior, and to
strengthen their positive involvement in the program.

Selection of Pupils

The fourth and fifth grades were selected to
participate in the program. The age level of these
two grades represents a period of particular interest
in child development. The two grades mark the child's
entrance into the upper years of elementary school.
Jenkins et al. state that in interests the fourth
grader is closer to the fifth grader than to children
in lower grades.[1] The fourth grader is beginning to
think more for himself and to develop his own ideas
and point of view. The fifth grader is rounding out
his childhood and is becoming more aware of differences among people. His ideas are broadening, and
he is very interested in people, his community, and
world affairs.

Introduction of the Program to Pupils

The pupils were introduced to the program by
their individual teachers. The program was presented as a part of the social studies course area
in which pupils would be taking a series of trips
to different museums to learn more about New York
City. In those classes participating in interracial
activity, the teachers explained that the pupils
would be joining another class from a different
school. No mention was made of the racial composition of the other class.

Involvement of Parents

The investigator discussed the question of involvement of parents with the principal of each school. It was decided that a meeting with the parents of pupils in the study would be impractical. School procedures required that parents give written permission for each school trip and this was followed in the Activity Group Program. The investigator pointed out the perfunctory nature of this approval. Consequently, the principals agreed to send a message to the parents stating that their children would be involved in a special trip program and that the principals would be available to discuss the program with parents. In addition, plans were set up to seek the cooperation of parents in accompanying the children during the trips. Teachers were to make special efforts to request parents' presence on the trips.

SELECTION AND INVOLVEMENT OF TRIP SITE PERSONNEL

Factors in the Selection of Trip Sites

The investigator met with the administrators of the participating schools to discuss the selection of trip sites. The administrators had extensive knowledge of trip sites. With their experience in schools they had great understanding of children's needs and interests. They were fully familiar with curriculum at all grade levels. The investigator used these resources of the administrators to answer the following questions:

(a) Which trips were most pertinent in terms of their relationship to the pupils' curriculum?

(b) Which trips were of most interest to the pupils?

(c) Which trips had the school planned within its regular trip program? (This was ascertained to avoid repetition of trips in the Activity Group Program.)

(d) Which trips would provide a variety of experiences in which pupils could interact in different ways?

(e)   Which trips would provide opportunity for informal, satisfying interaction?

(f)   Which trips would be considered valuable by the teachers of the participating classes?

Adequate facilities at the trip site was a con-sideration, since some of the activities during the program--lunch and discussion--required a private area for the pupils.

The unique characteristics of the program, such as interracial partners, varied activities, and need for space required particular cooperation from trip site officials. The museum had to provide private areas and guides had to be alerted. Since many other schools visited the museums and made reserva-tions, the schedule for the Activity Group Program had to be set up months in advance. Thus it was im-portant to select trip sites represented by museum officials, guides, etc., who were cooperative and committed to the goals of the Activity Group Program.

The location of the trip sites in relation to both schools became a practical consideration. The trip sites had to be reasonably accessible, so that travel time would not be a burden. For example, since the participating schools were in the Bronx and Manhattan, trip sites in Brooklyn were not con-sidered.

The investigator met with many museum directors to discuss the needs and goals of the program. After reviewing many museums, three trip sites were se-lected that fulfilled the physical space needs of the program and were represented by personnel who were interested in the program and ready to provide com-plete support and cooperation. The trip sites se-lected were the Museum of the City of New York, the New York Botanical Gardens, and the Hispanic Society of America and the American Numismatic Society.

Liaison with Trip Sites

The curator or assistant curator was the museum official who met with the investigator to organize the trip program. The investigator met several times with each museum official prior to the trips to work out problems of organization. Trip schedules, some more than two months in advance, were set. Plans for the trip day were organized. Specific displays and

areas of interest were included as part of the
pupils' activities. Guided tours were arranged and
a time schedule for the trip day was established.
Arrival at the museums, guided tours, lunch, and discussions were all scheduled. Spaces--in some cases
four different areas on the same trip day--were made
available for lunch and discussions. The museum
officials were of invaluable aid, always being available during the Activity Group Program to make any
changes due to unexpected developments, such as
inclement weather or time pressures.

DESCRIPTION OF EXPERIMENTAL PROCEDURE

Experimental Procedure

All classes were pretested before the program*
with the Attitude Scale, the Social Distance Scale,
and the Projective Picture Test. These were followed by tests related to perceptions of classroom
experience: My Teacher, Classroom Life, How This
Class Thinks, and How I Feel About Others. A week
before the trips, all classes received the same introduction to the Activity Group Program, with vari-
ations according to the different types of interracial contact, from the individual teachers. Prior
to the first trip, each pupil was assigned a partner
of similar sociometric status on the basis of data
from the sociometric test How I Feel About Others.
These assignments remained the same during the three
trips and discussions. The procedure called for a
pair of classes from each school to visit the trip
facility on the same day. In the joint arrangement,
the classes participated together with inter-class
partners. In the separate arrangement, the classes
participated separately with intra-class partners.

Two fourth-grade classes, one from School A and
one from School B, and two fifth-grade classes, one
from School A and one from School B, were designated
J-J groups (Table 2). The procedure for the J-J
classes was joint trip and joint discussion. The
fourth and fifth grades went on separate days. They
arrived at the trip facility accompanied by their
teachers. The discussion leader joined the classes.

---

*Tables 1 and 2 in this section present the
experimental procedure.

TABLE 1

Experimental Procedure Used for Fourth and Fifth
Grades from Schools A and B

Experimental Groups	Pre Test	Types of Interracial Contact	Data Collected at Trip Site	Post Test
J-J	X	Joint Trips Joint Discussions	Y	Z
J-S	X	Joint Trips Separate Discussions	Y	Z
S-J	X	Separate Trips Joint Discussions	Y	Z
S-S	X	Separate Trips Separate Discussions	Y	Z

X = The Attitude Scale
    The Social Distance Scale
    The Projective Picture Test
    My Teacher
    Classroom Life
    How This Class Thinks
    How I Feel About Others

Y = Trip Rating Sheet
    Teacher-Discussion Leader Rating Sheet
    Discussion Leaders' Observational Material
    Teacher Observational Material

Z = The Attitude Scale
    The Social Distance Scale
    The Projective Picture Test

The teachers assigned the pupils to their inter-class partners and classes proceeded through the trip facility together. They ate lunch together with the pupil partners sitting next to each other. After lunch the pupils were given the Trip Rating Sheet. This concluded the Trip Activity.

TABLE 2

Fourth- and Fifth-Grade Class Assignments
to Experimental Treatments

| School | Grade | | Experimental |
	Fourth	Fifth	Treatment
A	4-1	5-1	J-J
B	4-1	5-1	J-J
A	4-2	5-2	J-S
B	4-2	5-2	J-S
A	4-3	5-3	S-J
B	4-3	5-3	S-J
A	4-4	5-4	S-S
B	4-4	5-4	S-S

With the same partners, the pupils then participated in the Discussion Activity. With the teacher acting as observer, the discussion leader introduced the activity and directed the pupils to record what they liked best on the trip. When this information was collected, the pupils were instructed to discuss the trip with their partners. They were to agree on the one aspect they liked the best, and to decide which one of them would report this to the whole group. After the pupil-partner discussions, a pupil from each pair reported. The teachers recorded the identity of the reporter and the content of the report. Thereafter, the pupils again filled out the Trip Rating Sheet and the Teacher-Discussion Leader Rating Sheet. The classes then returned to their respective schools.

The procedure for the J-S classes was joint trip and separate discussion. Two fourth-grade classes and two fifth-grade classes, one of each

from School A and School B, were designated as J-S
groups. The J-S classes followed the same procedure
as the J-J classes. At the conclusion of the Trip
Activity, the classes separated and went to different
assigned areas for the Discussion Activity with intra-
class partners. Separate discussion leaders led the
discussions, following the procedure outlined for the
Discussion Activity.

The procedure for the S-J classes was separate
trip and joint discussion. Two fourth-grade classes
and two fifth-grade classes, one each from School A
and School B, were designated as S-J groups. The
S-J classes arrived at the trip facility accompanied
by their teachers. Discussion leaders joined the
classes. The teachers assigned the pupils to their
intra-class partners and classes proceeded through
the trip facility separately. They ate lunch separately with the pupil partners sitting next to each
other. After lunch the pupils were given the Trip
Rating Sheet. This concluded the Trip Activity.
The two classes then came together to participate in
the Discussion Activity and the teachers assigned the
pupils to their inter-class partners. The discussion
leader led the discussion, following the procedure
outlined for the Discussion Activity.

The procedure for the S-S classes was separate
trip and separate discussion. Once more, two fourth-
grade classes and two fifth-grade classes, one from
each school, were designated as S-S groups. The S-S
classes arrived at the trip facility accompanied by
their teachers. The discussion leaders joined the
classes. The teachers assigned the pupils to their
intra-class partners. Each class then separately
followed the same procedure outlined for the Trip
and Discussion Activities.

This procedure was repeated three times for each
class, once for each trip. At the conclusion of all
the trips, the attitude tests--the Attitude Scale,
the Social Distance Scale, and the Projective Picture
Test--were readministered. Three months had elapsed
since the tests had been administered the first time.

Table 2 presents the treatment assignments of
the fourth- and fifth-grade classes in the Activity
Group Program. Each of the four experimental treatments included a pair of fourth-grade classes and a
pair of fifth-grade classes. In this way the effects

of the Activity Group Program could be observed on two grade levels.

To facilitate interaction, classes assigned to the same experimental treatment were matched according to reading ability. Classes with the highest reading levels were assigned to the treatments with the greatest interracial contact.

Selection of Instruments

The selection of attitude measures for the study was determined by four factors: previous successful use with children, ease of reading, interest level, and an effort to include a variety of tests.

The investigator selected a battery of three tests--the Attitude Scale, the Social Distance Scale, and the Projective Picture Test--that met these criteria. They were previously used successfully with children. They held the interest of the children and were easy to read. The tests use a variety of approaches. One of the tests--the Projective Picture Test--is more disguised in its approach. It uses photographs and makes no mention of racial groups.

Description of Subjects

Of the 477 pupils initially tested, 243 were retained as subjects.* The other 234 were eliminated from the study because of failure to attend all three trips, parental objection to the tests, absence from tests, or ethnic background (Table 3).

Practically equal numbers of Negro and white pupils, and fourth- and fifth-grade pupils, participated in the study. More girls than boys were included in the program (Table 4).

Reading achievement for the subjects is based on the Metropolitan Reading Test. Form B of the Elementary Reading Test was administered to fourth-grade pupils. Form Bm of the Intermediate Reading Test was administered to the fifth-grade pupils.

Since the fourth-grade classes were grouped according to reading achievement, there were

---

*See Tables 3, 4, and 5 in this section.

TABLE 3

Pupils Eliminated from Study

School	Transfer	Absences Test	Absences Trip	Parental Refusal	Ethnic Background Puerto Rican	Ethnic Background Chinese	Ethnic Background Negro	Ethnic Background White
A	1	42	40	0	17	0	0	0
B	7	36	48	4	7	1	31	0
Total	8	78	88	4	24	1	31	0

TABLE 4

Pupils in Activity Group Program
by Grade, Sex, and School

Grade	Sex	School A Negro Pupils	School B White Pupils
4-1	Boys	6	10
	Girls	13	11
	Total	19	21
4-2	Boys	7	8
	Girls	9	5
	Total	16	13
4-3	Boys	5	10
	Girls	12	6
	Total	17	16
4-4	Boys	5	7
	Girls	9	5
	Total	14	12
4 Totals	Boys	23	35
	Girls	43	27
	Total	66	62
5-1	Boys	9	8
	Girls	9	13
	Total	18	21
5-2	Boys	7	6
	Girls	9	8
	Total	16	14
5-3	Boys	5	4
	Girls	4	9
	Total	9	13
5-4	Boys	6	9
	Girls	6	3
	Total	12	12
5 Totals	Boys	27	27
	Girls	28	33
	Total	55	60

TABLE 5

Intercorrelations of Reading Scores and Age of Fourth and Fifth
Grade Negro and White Experimental Subjects

Variable	1	2	3
	Negro		White
1. Word Knowledge	—	+.831*(4th) +.702*(5th)	+.101(4th) -.445*(5th)
2. Reading	+.911*(4th) +.775*(5th)	—	-.188(4th) -.212(5th)
3. Age	-.079(4th) -.232(5th)	-.058(4th) -.158(5th)	—

*Significant at the .01 level

significant differences in reading scores among the
fourth-grade experimental groups within each race
(Appendix A). Comparisons between the races in the
same experimental treatment reveal that fourth-grade
Negro and white pupils showed no significant differences in reading with the one exception of the S-J
treatment group for Word Knowledge (at the .01 level,
Appendix A).

There were no significant differences in age
among fourth-grade experimental groups within each
race, nor between races in the same experimental
groups (Appendix B).

Since the fifth-grade classes were grouped
according to reading achievement, there were significant differences in reading scores among the fifth-
grade experimental groups within each race (Appendix
A). Comparisons between the races in the same experimental treatments reveal that fifth-grade Negro
and white pupils had significant differences in Word
Knowledge and Reading scores (Appendix A).

There were no significant differences in age
between fifth-grade Negro and white pupils in the
same experimental groups. Age comparisons among
fifth-grade experimental groups within each race reveal significant differences between J-J and S-S
groups for both races and J-S and S-S groups for
Negro pupils (Appendix B).

Pearson Product-Moment Correlation Coefficients
were calculated between reading scores and age
(Table 5). For Negro and white fourth- and fifth-
grade pupils, the two reading scores, Word Knowledge
and Reading, were highly correlated. Fourth-grade
Negro pupils had a higher correlation, .911, compared
with .755 for fifth-grade Negro pupils. Fourth-grade
white pupils also had a higher correlation, .831,
compared with .702 for fifth-grade white pupils.
Age was not correlated with either reading score for
fourth-grade Negro or white pupils. For fifth-grade
white pupils age and Word Knowledge had a correlation
of -.445.

SUMMARY

This chapter presented a description of the following aspects of the activity group program: the
selection and involvement of school personnel; the

selection of trip sites; the organization of group
activities in the experimental program; the selection of attitude measures; and the nature of the
subjects.

The principals in the selected schools expressed
an interest in experimentation, a personal commitment
to the goals of the program, and a readiness to cooperate in implementing the research. More than a
majority of the pupils in each school (85 percent)
represented a different racial group. The principals'
evaluations were used to select teachers. The selected teachers were judged to be emotionally mature,
willing to participate in an experimental program,
and unprejudiced. The discussion leaders in the
study had at least three years of teaching experience
in the grade levels used in the study. The leaders
showed interest in the program and demonstrated the
required skills for conducting discussions. Fourth-
and fifth-grade pupils were selected to participate
in the study since pupils in the two grades share
common interests.

Various methods were used to involve teachers
and discussion leaders in the activity group program. Meetings were held to orient teachers and
discussion leaders to the procedures and goals of
the program, to present and analyze teacher and discussion leader roles, and to discuss the influence
of teachers' and discussion leaders' interracial
attitudes on pupils in the study. Role-playing experiences were used to develop practices and skills
necessary to communicate the social norm supportive
of friendly interracial pupil contact. Discussion
leaders had the added experience of participation in
a series of observer training exercises to develop
uniform, objective standards for recording behavior
during the Activity Group Program.

Steps were taken to involve parents and pupils
in the program. Each principal described the program to parents and invited them to discuss the program with him. Teachers urged parents to accompany
pupils on the trips. Pupils received an introduction to the program describing it as a series of
social studies activities in conjunction with another
school.

School administrative problems in relation to
the program--trip schedules, teacher meetings,

testing programs, and trip transportation--were
managed with the help of the assistant principals.

The selected trip sites provided a variety of
experiences appropriate to the needs and interests
of the pupils. The personnel of the trip sites expressed a commitment to the goals of the research
program and a readiness to cooperate in its imple-
mentation. During the program, organizational problems involving the trip sites--schedules, guided
tours, museum activities, allocation of physical
space--were solved with the aid of the museum curator
or assistant curator.

The experimental procedure in the Activity Group
Program involved the manipulation of partner assignments in Trip and Discussion Activities to produce
the following four types of interracial contact:
(1) the J-J treatment, consisting of interracial
partner assignments between schools during both Trip
and Discussion Activities; (2) the J-S treatment,
consisting of interracial partner assignments between schools during the Trip Activity and same race
partner assignments within a class during the Discussion Activity; (3) the S-J treatment, consisting
of same race partner assignments within a class during the Discussion Activity; and (4) the S-S treatment, consisting of same race partner assignments
within a class during both the Trip and Discussion
Activities. There was a different fourth- and fifth-
grade class from each school in each experimental
treatment. Partner assignments were based on sociometric test results and were of the same grade, sex,
and relative popularity status.

The Trip Activity included the first part of
the trip day. It consisted of arrival at the museum,
assignment of partners, viewing of museum displays,
and lunch with pupil partners. The Discussion
Activity included the second part of the trip day.
It consisted of a discussion between partners in
which pupils shared what they liked best about the
trip, came to an agreement on what was best, and
decided which pupil would report to the whole group.

The three attitude instruments--Attitude Scale,
Social Distance Scale, and Projective Picture Test--
had been previously used with children. Children
found them interesting and easy to read. One of the
tests--the Projective Picture Test--was disguised in

its approach, using photographs and making no reference to racial groups.

The 243 pupils in the study were in classes
according to reading level. Classes in the same
treatments were matched in reading ability. In both
grades there were significant reading differences
between the treatment groups in the same school as
well as between the same treatment groups in different schools. The only significant difference in age
was among fifth-grade classes in the same schools.
The two reading measures, Word Knowledge and Reading
showed high positive correlations for Negro and
white fourth- and fifth-grade pupils. The only
significant correlation between age and reading
ability was the negative correlation between age
and Word Knowledge for fifth-grade white pupils.

NOTES

1. Gladys G. Jenkins, Helen S. Shacter, and
William W. Bauer, These Are Your Children (Chicago:
Scott, Foresman, 1966).

CHAPTER **5** PROCEDURES USED
IN COLLECTING
DATA

The racial attitudes of the subjects were
measured with three tests which have been used for
this purpose with elementary school children: the
Attitude Scale, the Social Distance Scale, and the
Projective Picture Test.

THE ATTITUDE SCALE

The Attitude Scale* was developed by Gough,
Harris, Martin, and Edwards in their study with public school children.[1] The test includes eighteen
items, twelve favorable and six unfavorable. Subjects are directed to agree or disagree with each
statement.

THE SOCIAL DISTANCE SCALE

The Social Distance Scale* was developed by
Bogardus,[2] who described it as follows:

> The social distance approach may be
> viewed as a form of sociometrics in
> which attention is centered on the
> measurement of personal-group rela-
> tions, on the measurement of changes
> in these relations, on the use of
> stereotypes in such measurement, and
> on attempts to utilize feeling re-
> actions as a means of understanding
> human behavior.[3]

---

*See Appendix C for test data and administra-
tion procedures.

The Social Distance Scale consists of nine statements about members of a specified group. The subjects are directed to indicate their willingness or unwillingness to accept members of a group in nine different situations or relationships ranging from less intimate (e.g., visit our country) to the very intimate (e.g., be willing to marry one of them when I grow up).

THE PROJECTIVE PICTURE TEST

The Projective Picture Test* was developed by Radke, Sutherland, and Rosenberg in their study with Negro and white children.[4] The test involves the assignment of behavioral characteristics to a series of photographs of Negro and white children (eight Negro boys, eight Negro girls, eight white boys, and eight white girls) which are projected on a screen in four slides of eight pictures each. Each slide has two boys and two girls of each racial group placed in two rows with race and sex alternated; the photographs are lettered from A to H. Each position is taken by a different sex and race on each of the four slides. The slides are shown in the order: IV, I, II, III, IV, I, II, etc. (IV is given first as a practice situation).

A different behavioral description is presented orally with each slide and the subjects are asked which child in the slide is being described. Twenty-four behavioral descriptions are used, twelve positive and twelve negative. The subjects are thus required to select a Negro or white photograph, identified by a letter from A through H, in response to a descriptive statement.

SUPPLEMENTARY TESTS

The investigator collected data about the pupils' perceptions of their own classes to explain racial attitude changes during the activity group program. Pupils have feelings about many aspects of classroom life. Since a pupil's feelings toward his class may

---

*See Appendix C for test data and administration procedures.

influence his reaction to the activity group program, the subjects' perceptions of their class' social and emotional atmosphere were gathered.

Three tests were used to measure pupil perception of class social and emotional atmosphere: My Teacher, Classroom Life, and How This Class Thinks. The tests were developed at the Institute for Social Research, University of Michigan.[5] None of the instruments was standardized.

My Teacher

My Teacher* consists of ten descriptive phrases of the teacher. Each concerns such dimensions as teacher direction in school work and behavioral areas, teacher concern with pupil self-responsibilities, and teacher expression of affect in relation to the pupils. For each phrase the subject chooses from a series of options, including the desire that the teacher change in a greater direction, that the teacher remain the same, or that the teacher change in a lesser direction.

Classroom Life

Classroom Life* consists of seven incomplete thoughts that the subject must complete or answer about life in the classroom in terms of cooperation, friendliness, interest, and involvement in work. The subject has a choice of responses to select from for each item.

How This Class Thinks

How This Class Thinks* consists of seven statements about pupil participation and cooperation, teacher expectations for pupils, and teacher understanding of pupils. The subject indicates his estimate of how many pupils in the class are in agreement with each statement.

RATING SHEETS

To determine the subjects' perceptions of the activity group program, the investigator devised

---

*See Appendix C for test data and administration procedures.

two rating sheets, the Trip Rating Sheet and the
Teacher-Discussion Leader Rating Sheet.

The Trip Rating Sheet

The Trip Rating Sheet* consists of three questions to determine the pupils' feelings about the
Activity Group Program in general and about their
partners in particular. The subjects respond by
choosing one of several answers.

The Teacher-Discussion Leader
Rating Sheet

The Teacher-Discussion Leader Rating Sheet*
consists of two questions to determine the pupils'
feelings about the roles of the teacher and discussion leader in the Activity Group Program. The subjects respond by choosing one of several given
answers.

OBSERVATIONAL MATERIAL

To gather information on pupil interaction and
teacher behavior during the Activity Group Program,
observational techniques were used. Discussion
leaders and teachers acted as observers.

PARENT REACTION

A record was kept of parent responses to the
Activity Group Program that were expressed in meetings with the principals, teachers, or discussion
leaders.

NOTES

1. Harrison G. Gough et al., "Children's Ethnic
Attitudes: I. Relationship to Certain Personality
Factors," Child Development, XXI (1950), 83-91.

---

*See Appendix C for test data and administra-
tion procedures.

2.   Emory S. Bogardus, "Measuring Social Distance," Journal of Applied Sociology, IX (1925), 299-308.

3.   Emory S. Bogardus, "Measurement of Personal-Group Relations," Sociometry, X (1947), 306.

4.   Marian Radke, Jean Sutherland, and Pearl Rosenberg, "Racial Attitudes of Children," Sociometry, XIII (1950), 154-71.

5.   Institute for Social Research, Inventory of Classroom Study Tools for Understanding and Improving Classroom Learning Processes (Ann Arbor: University of Michigan Press, 1962).

6

This chapter presents a description of the behavior of pupils, teachers, and parents during the activity group program.

PUPIL BEHAVIOR

Joint-Joint Classes (Fourth Grade)

Class 4-1* from School A (Negro) arrived at the museum. The weather was mild and since the class from School B (white) had not yet arrived, the Negro pupils went across the street to Central Park. The pupils were well dressed. They were enthusiastic but well behaved. The girls walked arm in arm and the boys joked together. The class was an IGC group, Intellectually Gifted Children. The pupils walked in line and seemed to know exactly what to do without direction from the teacher. One of the pupils sketched idly while the class waited in the park. The teacher commented proudly and affectionately, "Talent."

The Negro class came back from the park when the white class was seen approaching the museum. The pupils from both classes were hesitant when they saw each other for the first time. One girl from the Negro class commented, "I'm not going to hold hands with those kids," when she saw the white pupils. The pupils from the two classes eyed each other guardedly. Slowly, as all the pupils realized they were going through the museum together, there seemed to be an increase in tension within each class. Boys from both

---

*Interracial trip and interracial discussion contact.

classes stared at each other. Girls talked nervously
with their classmates.

The pupil partner assignments were called out
by the teacher. The children lined up so that a
Negro child was standing next to his white partner.
Contact between races was variable. Some pupils
quickly interacted easily and pleasantly with their
partners. For the most part, though, the pupils
accompanied their partners quietly. Many pupils
attempted to talk with friends from their own classes.

As the classes went through the museum together,
white children more frequently turned away from their
Negro partners to talk to white classmates. The
Negro pupils seemed more open to interracial contact
than white pupils. A number of Negro boys were in
animated conversations with their white partners.
Two or three Negro girls were holding hands with their
white partners. One of these was the same Negro girl
who had commented earlier that she wouldn't hold
hands.

At the various window displays, many of the
children left their partners and clustered together
with their classmates. More white children than
Negro pupils responded to questions posed by the
quide.

At lunch partners sat next to each other. Interaction between races was limited. A number of boys
were joking with their partners. One of the Negro
boys was telling his white partner about his team.
Many of the girls sat next to their partners eating
without talking. A few girls were having lively conversations with their partners. During the discussion the children talked enthusiastically with their
partners. They seemed to enjoy sharing their reactions to the trip.

At the second contact, the New York Botanical
Gardens, the pupils from both classes seemed genu-
inely pleased to see each other. There was a great
deal of friendly interaction. There was much less
self consciousness and hesitancy. As the children
moved through the exhibits, many of the partners
talked with each other. At one point, a white child
excitedly pointed out something to his Negro partner.
At another time, a Negro boy and a white boy playfully pulled at each other's jacket. A Negro girl
and her white partner held hands. A cluster of Negro

and white boys discussed one of the exhibits. A
Negro girl affectionately played with her white
friend's hair. An interracial group of girls giggled
together about each other's boyfriends.

At lunch, the positive interaction between Negro
and white pupils continued. Some boys playfully
interacted with their partners in mock fighting. A
number of pupils shared food. There were, however,
several pupils who turned and interacted with their
own classmates. During the Discussion Activity, the
pupils talked to their partners enthusiastically.

At the third contact, the Hispanic Society of
America, the partners immediately started to converse
in a friendly manner. Walking through the museum
building, many pupils started to gravitate toward
their own classmates. Most Negro boys walked along
quietly while the white boys talked excitedly among
themselves. There were a few instances of interaction between Negro and white girls, but most girls
conversed with their classmates.

At lunch, there was an increase in interclass
interaction. Among the boys there were many examples
of playful fighting. Some of the boys laughingly
threw salt at each other. Many Negro and white girls
giggled and talked together. The pleasant tone continued throughout the discussion.

At the end of the trip, both classes left the
museum on the same school bus. The bus took the
Negro children to the subway. It was a short trip
and there was very little interaction between classes.
When the Negro children got off the bus, the white
children waved goodbye.

Joint-Joint Classes (Fifth Grade)

Class 5-1* from School B (white) arrived by bus.
The pupils had to wait to enter the museum because
the other class was delayed in arriving. As time
passed the class was becoming somewhat restless. A
cluster of two or three girls gathered to quietly
sing together. The teacher did not disapprove of
this behavior. As the wait extended beyond fifteen

---

*Interracial trip and interracial discussion
contact.

minutes the teacher, apparently recognizing the restlessness of the pupils, formed a game of throwing a
ball at a coin placed in the crack of the pavement.
In fact, she became a participant playing opposite
one of the pupils.

When the Negro pupils arrived, there was a stir
from both classes as they realized they were going
to meet. The teacher of the Negro class spoke quietly
in getting her class ready for partner assignments.
She calmly urged her class to pay attention. The
teacher of the white class took charge and read out
the partner assignments in a firm, loud, and pleasant
voice. When the children heard their names called,
they left their classes and formed new lines next
to their new partners. The children did this rather
shyly; some looking guardedly at their partners;
others looking curiously at their new partners; and
others actively avoiding facing their partners. A
number of pupils from both classes searched around
for their friends in their own classes to see if they
could be near them. The children seemed surprised
and excited by this new arrangement.

After the partner assignments were made, the
pupils were led by the museum guides with the teachers
retiring into a secondary position. As the children
walked through the museum, there was limited between
class interaction. A few partners talked to each
other a great deal. Others said nothing to each
other. Most children, Negro and white, seemed unsure
of how to handle the situation. The pupils quietly
followed their guides from exhibit to exhibit. At
a number of display cases, several of the white girls
broke off from their Negro partners to join their
classmates.

At lunch each child sat next to his or her assigned partners. Before this was organized by the
teachers, some children, mainly white, tried to sit
next to their own classmates. As the children ate
their lunches, some children said nothing to their
partners. Others kept looking around for their own
classmates. A few turned around to another row to
talk to their friends. There were four or five
partner pairs who talked easily among themselves.
They seemed to be enjoying themselves. Some partners
laughingly shared parts of their lunch.

During the discussion after lunch, one of the
teachers moved the children in one row of seats to

another section. When she was questioned, she indicated that the girls had seen some roaches and rather
than cause any further upset she decided to move the
children quietly. The other pupils were busily
sharing reactions to the trip with their partners.

At the second trip experience, the white class
arrived a few minutes early. The children, neatly
lined up, waited on the Garden grounds. Shortly,
the Negro pupils arrived and started to approach the
white pupils. Many of the pupils from both classes
smiled and waved at each other. As the names were
read for the inter-class partner assignments, some
four or five from each class called out the names
of their partners. This was in sharp contrast to
the caution and guardedness exhibited at their first
meeting.

With their partners, the pupils moved to the
museum building. Although the partners started out
beside each other, there was hardly any interaction
during the walk. Self-consciousness and uncertainty
seemed to set in. Pupils started to look toward the
nearby pupil from their own class.

Gravitating toward a pupil from one's own class
occurred frequently throughout this trip experience.
As the pupils followed the guide, the organized pattern of each pupil next to his partner tended to
weaken. This was especially prevalent among the girls.
There was more intermingling between the Negro and
white boys.

After they had viewed the displays, the children
were led outside the building. During a short wait,
practically all of the Negro girls sat on one or two
benches, whereas the white girls sat on different
benches. Some of the Negro and white boys shared the
same benches.

As the children headed toward another building,
they walked alongside their partners. Some Negro
girls moved slightly away from their partners and
approached classmates. A few Negro girls started
singing a song and the white girls joined in until
both classes were singing together.

During lunch, although partners were sitting
next to each other, inter-class interaction was limited. Some pupils stretched out from their seats
to talk to pupils from their own class. The children

participated enthusiastically in the discussion following lunch. They enjoyed sharing the trip reactions with their partners.

When questionnaires were distributed to the
children to elicit trip reactions, one white boy
refused to fill it out saying, "My mother told me not
to take any more tests." This mother had previously
strongly objected to the principal concerning the
attitude tests the pupils took before the trip program began. She had been so upset about the nature
of the tests that she had insisted her son's test
papers be destroyed.

At the third trip experience, the classes arrived at about the same time. The white class was
accompanied by four parents whom the teacher introduced as members of the P.T.A. The large number of
parents and the fact that they were all P.T.A. members seemed unusual. The discussion leader had the
feeling that these white parents were in some way
checking up on what this Activity Group Program was
all about. There had been some reports that there
were parents in the white school concerned about the
program.

Many of the pupils seemed pleased to see each
other, smiling as they quickly moved alongside their
partners. This was particularly true of the Negro
girls. As they walked through the museum building,
though, pupils had little interaction with their
partners. Pupils turned toward their own classmates
and ignored their partners. Many of the Negro girls
started to complain of stomach aches. They frequently
asked when they could eat lunch. More and more children, Negro and white, grew restless. The teachers
were having difficulty keeping the children quiet and
orderly.

At lunch, a number of Negro girls tried to sit
next to their own classmates and responded angrily
when they were asked to return to their assigned
partners. A Negro and white boy started to fight.
When the pupils were asked to discuss the trip with
their partners, these two boys refused to talk to
each other. However, most partner pairs were talking calmly and pleasantly. When the discussion was
over and the classes left, some Negro and white
children exchanged goodbyes.

Joint-Separate Classes (Fourth Grade)

The weather was brisk as the two 4-2* classes
arrived at about the same time. Both groups of
children were well dressed. The children were alert
and energetic. Partner assignments were made in the
museum after the children had disposed of their
coats and lunches. At first, the children seemed
somewhat hesitant in joining the new partners. One
white girl loudly expressed dissatisfaction with
the idea of moving to a new partner. All the other
children quietly accepted the idea of joining the
new partner. One white girl took the hand of her
Negro partner, and started talking to her. The
white girl smilingly remarked to her teacher, "She's
in 4-2 like me." After the pupils walked together
for a few minutes through the museum, the atmosphere
between classes was markedly friendly. Practically
all the girls were holding hands and talking to each
other. A Negro and white girl sat in each other's
lap in the first room visited. During a guide's
lecture the same Negro girl put her head in the white
girl's lap for the entire time. The white girl accepted this quite naturally. Another Negro girl
listened to a guide's talk with her arm resting on
her white partner's shoulder.

The boys were less involved in interacting with
their partners. Their attention focussed more on the
museum displays. Some of the white boys left their
partners and started taking notes on pads they had
brought. More boys asked questions of the museum
guides. There were a few instances of Negro and white
boys talking together in a friendly manner. At lunch
there was a pushing episode between a Negro and white
boy who were not partners.

At the second contact, it was a windy, chilly
day. The children were appropriately dressed except
for one Negro boy who had on only a heavy sweater.
The pupils were somewhat subdued as interclass partner
assignments were started. The children recognized
each other from the previous trip but not immediate
overt expressions of greeting or friendliness were
made. As the first group of children got together,
there were little giggles as they took a quick look

---

*Interracial trip contact and separate discus-
sion.

at each other and turned away. Several of the white
children eagerly asked if they would have their same
partners.

When the pupils went through the museum building,
some of the children drifted back to their own classmates. There were some examples of Negro and white
girls holding hands. One of the white girls was
chewing some candy drops. She gave candy to her
Negro partner as well as to some other Negro girls.
When the children left the museum building to walk
to another building, it was very windy and cold and
the pupils did not have an opportunity for much interaction. Some children walked alongside their partners. Others tried to walk with their own classmates.

At lunch, there was noisy talking among groups
of interracial partners. There were two or three
groups talking together--joking, teasing, and sharing
food. One white girl offered candy to her Negro
partner. A group of Negro and white boys were laughing playfully among themselves.

In a brief discussion after lunch, the pupils
were asked what they talked about with their partners.
Some responses from both Negro and white children
were: "We talked about what we saw in the museum;"
"I told my partner about fire drills in my school;"
"We compared bus passes;" "They think they can beat
us in punch ball;" and "They can't bring bottled soda
on the trip."

One white child in referring to her Negro partner started out by saying, "One of my friends. . ."

As the school bus carrying the white children
approached the Hispanic Society at the start of the
third trip, most of the Negro children who were
standing in line in front of the museum seemed pleased
to see the other class. Two Negro boys, however,
were overheard complaining, "Oh, that faggy class!
Do we have to go with them?"

The teacher paired the two classes and the Negro
and white pupils quickly began to converse with each
other as the groups started toward the museum. A
Negro boy told his white partner, "I don't like our
school. Too many bad children there." These
two boys walked arm in arm. Other Negro and white
boys excitedly discussed the exhibits together. There
was a great deal of casual talking, teasing, and

playful fighting among Negro and white pupils. Pupils from both schools helped each other select souvenir postcards.

During lunch, the positive contacts between Negro and white children continued. There were numerous examples of Negro and white pupils laughing, sharing food, and playing together.

Joint-Separate Classes (Fifth Grade)

Both 5-2 classes* arrived at the museum at about the same time. The children looked curiously. As the partner assignments were called out, several Negro and white pupils refused to join their new partners. With some mild teacher insistence, the pupils moved to their partners. The tone between classes was somewhat strained as they entered the museum. The pupils talked mainly to their own classmates even though they walked beside their new partners.

The classes were led by a guide through various display areas. Interracial contact slowly developed. Some of the more outgoing Negro boys talked easily with their white partners. A Negro and white girl were holding hands. When the guide described how hard children worked in colonial days, a white girl enthusiastically commented to her Negro partner, "Poor thing." Both girls seemed sad about the hardships the colonial children faced. More girls were talking to and enjoying their partners.

In one of the exhibition rooms the children were asked to sit down. Two white girls refused to sit next to their partners. The girls said they were friends since the first grade, and furthermore the Negro girls "don't want to sit with us anyhow." Other partners sat next to each other and listened to the guide.

During lunch the pupils talked quietly and the room atmosphere was pleasant. The same white girls who had earlier refused to sit next to their Negro partners now sat next to their Negro partners conversing in a friendly manner. One Negro boy did a

------

*Interracial trip contact and separate discussion.

finger trick and soon the whole row of boys was
talking and comparing tricks. After lunch on the
way out, a Negro girl was overheard saying, "My
partner's name is Wendy. She was so nice."

At the second trip, the day was sunny and brisk.
It was an ideal autumn day. The white pupils arrived
a few minutes early. As the Negro pupils approached,
a white girl said loudly to her classmates, "Put on
your gloves, we'll have to hold their hands." This
remark seemed to reflect the feelings of many white
girls toward the Negro girls throughout the trip.
Overtly and subtly the white girls expressed hostility.

The pupils joined their partners without making
any comments. There was very little interaction
between partners. Pupils tended to talk to their own
classmates. The girls, in particular, were reluctant
to talk to their assigned partners. As the pupils
walked through the museum building, pupils wandered
away from their partners. Clusters of classmates
formed. One white girl seemed to have a number of
followers in her class and she was particularly
opposed to being paired with her Negro partner. When
the pupils were reminded to accompany their partners
for about the fourth time, the same white girl turned
to a few classmates and mockingly said, "And what's
your name? And what's your name?" in a voice loud
enough for the Negro girls to hear. Her white followers promptly snickered. The Negro girls standing
nearby seemed to lower their heads.

There was more interaction between Negro and
white boys. The boys went to the lavatory and spent
about ten minutes there. When they came out, the
teacher commented that he should have left them there
because they were all having a good time swinging on
the bars extending from the wall.

At lunch, although partners sat next to each
other, there was limited contact between girl partners. One Negro girl shared food with her white
partner. Another pair of girls was overheard discussing the bedtimes. A number of white girls leaned
across to another row to talk to their own classmates.
Other girls just sat quietly and ate their lunch.
There was a little more contact among boy partners.

On the third trip, the Negro pupils arrived a
few minutes earlier than the white pupils. The

pupils were standing in front of the museum when
the school bus carrying the white children arrived.
A few Negro youngsters waiting on line muttered,
"Oh, we thought we were going on this trip alone.
We have to go with that class?"

The teachers paired the two classes but the
children talked mainly with friends from their own
class. In the museum building, the pupils were
given a guided tour by the assistant curator. The
pupils were quiet and attentive. There were some
Negro and white boys who talked together about the
glass displays. A number of white girls left their
partners to join their friends.

The pupils moved to the next building. On the
way, the Negro and white boys conversed together
informally. There was hardly any interracial contact
among the girls. In the museum a Negro boy* became
very upset and wanted to fight with another Negro
boy in his class. This incident occurred in a very
large room with many other visitors besides the
pupils. Many of the pupils were occupied in different parts of the room so that very few of the
pupils seemed aware of the incident. While the upset boy was led outside by his teacher, the pupils
continued to look at the displays. After a few minutes the classes lined up outside the building in
preparation for going to lunch. The Negro youngster
was still upset. He told his teacher that he would
kill that "white creep," a reference to the Negro
boy with whom he was angry. The teacher tried to
calm the youngster. Soon a few of the pupils became
aware of the cause of their wait. They watched a
policeman and the teacher physically assist the boy
into the teacher's car. A white boy commented, "Boy,
I never saw a policeman do that before!" The incident seemed quickly forgotten as the two groups moved
on to lunch. During lunch, the friendliest interaction between Negro and white pupils occurred. One
table of boys enthusiastically discussed their favorite baseball players. Other boys and girls talked
and laughed together.

---

*It was later discovered that he had previously
been identified by his school as seriously emotionally disturbed.

Separate-Joint Classes (Fourth Grade)

At the first trip, the two 4-3 classes* arrived separately. The white class came by bus and the Negro class walked to the museum.

The Negro pupils, among themselves, were animated and friendly. They walked arm-in-arm, talked enthusiastically about what they saw, and responded to questions from the guide. Three children were sucking their thumbs. The white children, among themselves, were quieter, less aggressive, and less friendly.

When the classes were brought together and the children were informed they were getting new partners, pupils in both classes tittered. They seemed nervous but yet were very interested in what was going to happen. After the teacher called a few names, a stout white child stood up to meet his Negro partner. A number of Negro children laughed loudly at him and started teasing him. He was called "white fat." The teacher quickly stopped the teasing and attempted to restore order. A Negro girl called the teacher's attention to another cluster of children; "Ooo, they're calling her names." A few Negro girls were laughing at a white girl, saying, "She's white." The white girl looked upset and dumbfounded. Another Negro girl cried out, "That's not nice calling her white. You'll get into a fight." Another white girl burst into tears, apparently as a result of teasing.

These events lasted about three or four minutes at the most. The teachers stopped the teasing and the pupils were seated next to their partners. The atmosphere was strained as the discussion activity began. Although there was some positive contact between partners, the interaction was generally somewhat tense. Mostly Negro pupils gave the reports for the partner team discussions. The reports ended and the pupils were becoming restless. The classes separated into units and departed.

On the second trip, the day was unusually sunny and mild. Both classes arrived within ten minutes

---

*Separate trip and interracial discussion contact.

of each other. The white pupils, among themselves,
were excited and well behaved as they observed the
different displays. There was much friendly interaction, with many of the pupils holding hands. The
Negro pupils, among themselves, sprawled out in a
line as they walked. Two boys were in charge of the
boys' line and this led to loud complaining and pushing. The rest of the boys protested that one of the
monitors was bullying them about getting into line.
Among the Negro girls there was much friendly contact. At times some pupils explored parts of the
grounds away from the rest of the class, ignoring
the teacher's presence.

When the classes met for the joint discussion,
the pupils were quiet as they surveyed each other.
Some complaints were heard from the white pupils
about having to move to the Negro partners. (In
conversation earlier with the teacher of the white
class, she indicated that her pupils had developed
a negative feeling toward the Negro pupils because
of the fighting during the first trip). There was
very little interaction between partners. The
white pupils seemed to express quiet discomfort and
unfriendliness. The pupils worked together quickly
and there was a minimal amount of friendly spontaneous interaction. When the discussion was over,
both classes left without farewells. The white
pupils seemed relieved and the Negro pupils seemed
curious about the experience.

On the third trip, the Negro pupils, among
themselves, were noisy and out of line. The boys,
in particular, were most difficult to organize. As
the class moved through the trip area, the pupils
laughed and played together. The white pupils,
under the stricter control of their teacher, were
more organized though still lively. There was much
friendliness as the children talked and laughed together.

When the classes met for the joint discussion,
the pupils observed each other cautiously. There
was some reluctance on the part of a few Negro girls
to join their partners. There was little spontaneous
interaction between partners. There were, however,
some pupils who seemed to be enjoying the discussion
with their partners. Most pupils interacted quickly
and without warmth. When the discussion was over,
both classes formed separate groups. Most pupils
occupied themselves with their classmates, but some

pupils smiled at their partners from the other class as they departed.

Separate-Joint Classes (Fifth Grade)

The Negro class of the 5-3 pupils* arrived in good spirits. They started the tour in a quiet manner. They reacted positively to the guide and seemed to enjoy themselves. There was a great deal of positive contact among the pupils, both verbal and physical. Many girls walked hand-in-hand. Boys walked with their arms around each other's shoulders.

The white pupils seemed interested and enjoyed the tour. There also was much positive interaction. Pupils were responsive to the teacher and guide.

When the classes met, the pupils from both classes seemed excited and pleased at meeting new partners. Ten to fifteen sets of partners were observed talking pleasantly. The tone between groups was relaxed and friendly. The pupils could have talked together longer if there had been more time.

At the second trip, the white pupils were excited but orderly. There was much friendly contact among the children--girls were holding hands, boys were talking and draping their arms over each other's shoulders. The Negro pupils also showed much friendliness among themselves. They shouted out questions to their teacher and clustered around her, some taking her hand.

At the meeting of the classes, the pupils eyed each other carefully. Some pupils hesitated in joining their partners from the other class. Once the inter-class assignments were made and the pupils were seated next to their partners, the pupils seemed reserved and self-conscious. When the discussions started between partners, the pupils seemed to be enjoying themselves. Most of the pupils who reported about the partner discussions were white pupils. One of the last white pupils to report was reluctant to stand up saying, "All of the ones that have stood up have been from our class." He indicated that it wasn't fair that only members of his class reported.

---

*Separate trip and interracial discussion contact.

He wanted boys and girls from the other class to
report also.

After the discussion both classes got their
coats and prepared to leave. Both classes left in
the same bus for a few minutes. Since the pupils
had boarded the bus by class units, pupils of the
same class were adjacent to each other. This resulted in interaction mainly within classes.

On the third trip, the same pattern continued.
Both classes showed very positive interaction within
their own classes. Both teachers seemed liked and
the tone in both classes was relaxed and pleasant.
When the classes met, the children became somewhat
self-conscious. Several pupils turned toward their
classmates instead of their assigned partners during
the informal conversation prior to the discussion.
There were a number of instances of positive interaction between partners. The pupils responded favorably to the discussion and seemed to enjoy the
conversations with their partners. When the classes
got up to leave, there were no spoken goodbyes although some pupils looked back to their partners.

Separate-Separate Classes* (Fourth Grade)

School A--Negro Pupils. The class was notable for
its lack of discipline during the first two trip
experiences. The pupils seemed disinterested in the
trip exhibits. They were constantly talking. The
girls laughed together; the boys engaged in pushing,
pulling, and fighting encounters. At times the
children seemed out of control. There was constantly
interaction, much of it negative.

On the third trip experience, due primarily to
the change in teachers, the class behaved in striking
contrast to the previous trips. They lined up
quietly and in an orderly fashion. They responded
to the teacher. The girls still talked among themselves, but in a more positive tone. The boys showed
more interest in the trip exhibits and were much less
pugnacious among themselves. In general, there was
a marked improvement in the tone of the interaction
among the pupils. The girls held hands or walked

---

*Separate trip and separate discussion.

arm-in-arm; the boys talked in moderate tones in small groups.

School B--White Pupils. The class,* during the three trip experiences, behaved in a quiet, orderly manner with periods of harmless, slight playfulness. The pupils talked among themselves in a friendly, relaxed manner. This relaxed tone seemed to be due mainly to the easy manner of the teacher. The class showed much positive interaction. The pupils showed interest in the museum exhibits and displays. They were responsive to the questions their teacher asked them.

Separate-Separate Classes* (Fifth Grade)

School A--Negro Pupils. The class arrived in an orderly fashion. The pupils were friendly toward each other and there always was a quiet buzzing among the children. They seemed interested in the exhibits. The boys seemed to enjoy each other. They laughed and joked together. The girls stayed together and talked in small groups. There were a number of girls holding hands. On the second trip the children displayed some quarrelling and fighting. Some of the girls started complaining about their partners. The boys started wandering about and fighting. The looser environment of the second trip, with open grounds and walks, led to more spontaneous outbursts. The third trip had characteristics of the earlier trips. The pupils were restless and noisy. They gave slight attention to the museum displays and often did not follow the teacher's directions. However, the interaction between the pupils was positive. The children seemed to enjoy themselves and the fighting previously observed did not occur.

School B--White Pupils. There was much good feeling expressed among the pupils. Not only did partners interact positively, but small clusters of pupils talked together in a friendly manner. This was particularly noticeable among the boys. Boys were observed with arms draped over the shoulders of their partners. The pupils showed enthusiasm over the exhibits. They were very involved in the different displays they saw.

---

*Separate trip and separate discussion.

This was the same pattern for the three trips. The pupils were excited about the different exhibitions. They buzzed among themselves. When the pupils had lunch together, they held animated conversations. They shared food and laughed together. During the discussion periods the pupils enjoyed discussing the trip with their partners. They showed pleasure in standing up and presenting their ideas to the entire group.

TEACHER BEHAVIOR

Joint-Joint Teachers* (Fourth Grade)

<u>School A--Teacher of Negro Pupils</u>. The teacher is a young white woman with two years' teaching experience. She revealed that she was quite pleased to be working with a bright class. She spoke of how alert and quick her pupils were and she seemed proud of their intelligence.

Her general manner was quiet and distant. Throughout the trips she was unenthusiastic and showed no particular interest in the museum activities. Her interactions with pupils in her own class were minimal, and nonexistent with the other class. For the most part, she stayed in the background and said nothing. However, she seemed to have established good control methods with her class, since they were well behaved without her directions. On one occasion, she reprimanded a pupil for his behavior by saying, "I don't know if you can go on these trips."

In general, her attitude toward the trip program was one of uninvolvement and quiet negativeness. She expressed doubts about the worth of the trip experiences. She made no attempt to explain or clarify the exhibits to the pupils. She stayed removed from the discussion leaders and the teacher of the other class. During one of the trips, she complained of the cold weather and the walking.

The following comment of the observer summarizes the behavior of the teacher: "Her lack of warmth

---

*Interracial trip and interracial discussion contact.

and her inability to extend herself to children or
adults did not enrich the experience for the pupils
of the classes."

School B--Teacher of White Pupils. The teacher is
a young white woman with five years' teaching experience. She was an energetic, enthusiastic person.
She expressed keen appreciation of the educational
value of the exhibits and displays and constantly
brought them to the pupils' attention. She commented frequently about some aspect of the exhibits
and posed stimulating, thoughtful questions about
the exhibits to the children.

She maintained firm control over the behavior
of her class. She reprimanded her pupils whenever
they tended toward the slightest disorder. When a
pupil from the class talked out of turn to his partner from the other class, she sharply reminded the
pupil to be quiet with a somewhat sarcastically-
toned remark, "Do you want to give the guided tour?"
She did, however, show interest in the Negro pupils.
On a number of occasions she included them in brief
discussions and generally showed positive feelings
toward them.

She was a capable, hard-working teacher, somewhat lacking in warmth. She expressed disapproval
of the other teacher's lack of involvement and negative attitude. At the conclusion of the trip program, she went around and collected the addresses
of the Negro pupils so that her pupils could start
a correspondence.

Joint-Joint Teachers* (Fifth Grade)

School A--Teacher of Negro Pupils. The teacher is
a young white woman with three years' teaching experience. She had a quiet manner but was closely
involved in the activities of her pupils. Physically
small and with a small voice, she kept the pupils
interested and organized. She drew the attention
of the pupils to the exhibits. The pupils seemed
to like her and were quite responsive to her comments. Time and again she asked the pupils questions

---

*Interracial trip and interracial discussion
contact.

about what they were seeing. She encouraged them to
read the captions under the various displays.

She had a pleasant manner. She showed interest
in the pupils of both classes, including both classes
in her comments and asking questions of pupils in
both classes. She kept the class organized with
partners next to each other.

In general, she had a quiet efficiency. During
the lunch periods, discussions, and museum activities, she helped organize both classes. The following observer comment summarizes her behavior: "She
had a quiet, positive attitude toward the museum
activities and pupils of both classes. I don't think
I heard her raise her voice once. But she seemed to
always be there to help and provide encouragement
when needed."

School B--Teacher of White Pupils. The teacher is a
young white woman with ten years' teaching experience.
She was energetic and forceful. She spoke in a vi-
brant, assertive voice. She showed affection to the
children when she fondly zippered the hood on the
coat of one of her pupils. She playfully participated in a game with the children outside of one of
the trip sites as the class waited.

As the children walked through the museum she
smilingly repeated the names of the Negro pupils out
loud. The Negro children proudly acknowledged their
names as they were called out.

She was strongly in control of the behavior of
her pupils. A few times she was sharp when the
pupils misbehaved. When the pupils became noisy,
she reprimanded them strongly by saying to one child,
"I'll send you back home, if you don't behave."

During the second trip she referred to one of
her absent pupils with the suggestion that the child
didn't come on this trip because of something having
to do with the Negro pupils. While she mentioned
this, she seemed evasive and refused to explain anything more about it.

At times she was brusque with the children and
other times warm and friendly. However, she tried
to make the trip experiences meaningful at all times
by drawing children's attention to exhibits.

Joint-Separate Teachers* (Fourth Grade)

School A--Teacher of Negro Pupils. The teacher is a
young white woman in her second year of teaching.
She was an enthusiastic, strong, and dynamic teacher.
She enjoyed her class and assumed authority without
any difficulty. She directed the pupils with short
commands that did not insult or threaten. When she
had the class get together or move into a new experience, she made sure the pupils were quiet and in
order.

She was enthusiastic about the total project.
The responses and interest of her class indicated
that she had used preliminary material to prepare
her class for the trip experiences. During the trips
she attempted to increase her pupils' involvement by
reading and explaining exhibit captions. She seemed
proud of the responses of her pupils. Furthermore,
she seemed to find the material at the trip sites
fascinating herself.

In general, she had a very positive approach.
For example, during a discussion about the trip held
after the classes had separated, some of the pupils
started to voice negative ideas about their other
class partners. She tactfully encouraged the children to express what they liked about these partners.

School B--Teacher of White Pupils. The teacher is
a young white woman in her third year of teaching.
She had a relaxed, easy manner. She was always
aware of what was going on, but only stepped in when
it was necessary. When the pupils were tired and
restless at the end of the day, she was forceful and
strongly in control of the children.

She showed great interest in the entire project
and was particularly involved in the exhibitions and
displays of the museums. She actively involved her
pupils in the trip experiences by pointing out things
and posing questions to the children about what they
were seeing.

An example of her efforts to help with the trip
program was her pressing her sister into service to

----

*Interracial trip contact and separate discus-
sion.

accompany her class on one of the trips when a parent
who had promised to come failed to appear.

Joint-Separate Teachers* (Fifth Grade)

School A--Teacher of Negro Pupils. The teacher is a
young white man of five years' teaching experience.
He took an active interest in the trip program. He
encouraged his pupils to attend to various exhibits
and the guided talks.

He was quietly firm in maintaining behavioral
standards. He was calm and patient and the children
were responsive to his directions. He knew when to
be firm and when to be permissive. When the children
had to wait until the projector was repaired during
a film, he allowed them to talk and stand up understanding their restlessness. However, another time
when a white boy started fighting, he simply took the
boy's hand and walked him away. On the third trip
he effectively dealt with a difficult situation when
one of his pupils had a serious emotional outburst.
He walked the pupil away from both classes until the
pupil became less excited. Finally, he had the pupil
returned to school before the trip day was over.

On the second trip, the class was accompanied
by a substitute teacher. The substitute, a retired
fireman, was known to the pupils since he had sub-
stituted frequently in the school. He had a down-
to-earth, man-to-man approach to the pupils. He was
warm and gentle and pointed out various aspects of
the exhibits to the pupils. The children liked him
and felt comfortable with him.

School B--Teacher of White Pupils. The teacher is a
young Negro man of ten years' teaching experience.
He seemed uninvolved with his pupils and the trip
activity. He spoke in a low, flat voice. The only
observable contacts he had with the pupils were to
reprimand, threaten, or make a negative comment. He
made numerous denigrating comments about his class:
"They're so thick that I wonder if anything will
penetrate . . . ;" "Act like human beings;" "They're
supposed to be the second brightest, but . . . ;"

---

*Interracial trip contact and separate discus-
sion.

and "You'll never make it;" to a child who asked about college.

The teacher stayed in the background during the trips. He seemed annoyed by the whole activity. At the conclusion of the last trip, he expressed relief that the trips were over.

Separate-Joint Teachers* (Fourth Grade)

<u>School A--Teacher of Negro Pupils</u>. The teacher is a young white woman in her second year of teaching. She emerged as a passive, disinterested, quietly uncooperative teacher. Throughout the trips she hardly spoke. One observer commented; "I don't remember hearing her speak for the whole trip." Her control of her class was practically nonexistent. She seemed uninvolved with the pupils, their activities, and their trip experiences. At times the children became quite noisy and uncontrolled. Aside from an occasional half-hearted attempt to stop some children from fighting, she just ignored the behavior and made no attempt to create order. She seemed quite disorganized, failing to bring partner lists and material describing the trip sites.

<u>School B--Teacher of White Pupils</u>. The teacher is a young white woman with three years' teaching experience. She stayed in close contact with her class. She was constantly reminding the children to stay in line and to be quiet, using a loud, sharp voice which often became a shout. She rarely smiled at the pupils and her facial expression was generally, "You'd better behave."

She participated fully in the trip activities with an efficient, professional bearing. She carried the material describing the trip sites. At times she allowed the pupils to explore the exhibits by themselves. After a few minutes, she would call the pupils back and then, making sure that all the pupils could see her, proceeded to tell them more about the exhibits they had just observed.

She indicated concern at some of the unruliness of the Negro pupils and their teacher's lack of effort to control the class.

---

*Separate trip and interracial discussion contact.

Separate-Joint Teachers* (Fifth Grade)

<u>School A--Teacher of Negro Pupils</u>. The teacher is a young white woman in her first year of teaching. She indicated great interest in the trip program. It was evident that she liked the pupils in her class and that she wanted them to gain educational benefit from the trips. Her control over the class was erratic. At times the children listened and followed her directions. Other times they didn't. She seemed in particular not to be able to handle the boys. However, she maintained her warm approach to the pupils, didn't lose her temper, and smiled easily.

She pointed out some of the interesting aspects of the exhibits. She encouraged the pupils to pay attention.

<u>School B--Teacher of White Pupils</u>. The teacher is a young Negro woman in her second year of teaching. She had a strong, vibrant manner and had firm control over the behavior of her pupils. The children responded quickly to her. At all times she was very much involved with her pupils and the situation. At every opportunity she used the displays at the trip sites for educational purposes. She read the captions under the exhibits and asked her pupils questions.

Her manner was pleasant but businesslike. There was a no-nonsense quality to the way she interacted with the pupils. At the same time, she showed interest in them. She was close to them at all times. She helped them open soda cans at lunch, and played a game with some pupils.

Separate-Separate Teachers** (Fourth Grade)

<u>School A--Teacher of Negro Pupils</u>. The class had several teachers during the time period of the Activity Group Program. Their first teacher resigned in the time period between the first and second trip. Then the class experienced a number of day-to-day substitute teachers. One of these day-to-day

---

*Separate trip and interracial discussion contact.

**Separate trip and separate discussion.

substitutes accompanied the class on the second trip.
By the time the class went on the third trip, they
had been assigned a new teacher.

The first teacher had minimal control over the
behavior of her class, at the best. The general
impression that she gave was one of helplessness in
being able to manage her class. On the trip she
drifted into the background, remained uninvolved,
and had practically no contact with the pupils.

For the second trip the class had a day-to-day
substitute teacher. This temporary teacher was an
inexperienced young white woman who did not know the
pupils. Generally, the pupils did not listen to her
and her control over their behavior was weak. There
were no attempts to vitalize or explain any of the
trip displays.

The third teacher had been the reading teacher
in the school. She had over ten years of teaching
experience and had gained a reputation in the school
as a firm disciplinarian. She maintained strong and
consistent control of the class. Whenever the pupils
became too noisy or strayed out of line, she sharply
reprimanded them. She frequently shouted at the
pupils. The pupils were quick to respond to her
directions. She showed interest in the museum displays and encouraged the pupils to pay attention.
With a camera that she had brought, she took photographs of the children during the trip day. These
photographs were later displayed on the class bulletin
board.

School B--Teacher of White Pupils. The teacher is a
young white woman of six years' teaching experience.
Her manner was calm and patient. In a quiet, uncom-
manding way she was in control of the situation and
very much involved with her pupils. She explained
each exhibit carefully. An example of this occurred
when the children showed interest in some paintings.
She said to them, "Goya tried to make figures funny
and El Greco made his figures long." She asked the
children questions about some of the exhibits. Her
manner of speaking was easy and accepting. It com-
municated a respect for the children. She praised
the pupils and made sure that they were attentive.
The children seemed to like her and they responded
to her directions. Some children offered her cookies
which she accepted.

Separate-Separate Teachers* (Fifth Grade)

School A--Teacher of Negro Pupils. The teacher is
a young white woman in her third year of teaching.
Generally, she was pleasant, seldom getting angry or
raising her voice. However, her class was noisy,
out of order, and verging on the chaotic at times.
She, herself, indicated that she couldn't control
the class. While maintaining this calm exterior,
she drifted into the background and participated
minimally in the activities. She let the pupils
move around as they pleased and made no attempt to
draw their attention to any of the displays or exhibits. The children paid little attention to her.
Whatever cooperation she got from the pupils came
from the girls.

School B--Teacher of White Pupils. The teacher is
a young white man in his third year of teaching. He
seemed to be actively annoyed with the trip program,
conveying an attitude that he was being imposed on.
He was quietly uncooperative concerning the partner
assignments. Contrary to the agreed plan, he led
the pupils to think that they could choose their own
partners. As a result the pupils were unhappy when
they were assigned the regular partners.

When his pupils asked questions, he reluctantly
answered them. His facial expression and remarks
bespoke impatience and sarcasm. He made no attempt
to bring the entire group's attention to the trip
exhibits. In dealing with the children's behavior,
he was inconsistent, shouting for quiet at times,
uncaring at other times.

PARENT BEHAVIOR

Various sources provided reports concerning
parent reaction to the activity group program.

Report of Principal of School B (White Pupils).

At the outset of the Activity Group Program the
principal of School B reported that several parents
had complained about the tests used to assess the

---

*Separate trip and separate discussion.

white children's attitudes toward Negroes. One parent indignantly insisted that her son's test materials be destroyed.

During the trip program the principal of School B further reported that the Parent Teachers Association requested that he meet with a group of parents who were concerned about the Activity Group Program. At the meeting the parents expressed a strong opposition to the program. They complained that the pupils from the two schools had been required to hold hands. The parents expressed fears that the program was really a preliminary to a bussing plan that would bring Negro children to their school. They also felt that their children were being used as "guinea pigs."

Report of Trip Observers

During one trip, the trip observers reported that four white parents, identified as members of the Parent Teachers Association from School B, accompanied the white class. The observer had the impression that the parents were not merely present as parents accompanying a class, but rather were present as representatives of the Parent Teachers Association evaluating the program.

Report of Test Administrator

At the post administration of the attitude tests after the conclusion of the trip program, the test administrator reported that a number of white children refused to take the tests saying, "My mother told me not to take the tests." Among these children were two fourth-grade pupils from the joint trip-joint discussion class and three fifth-grade pupils from the joint trip-joint discussion class.

CHAPTER 7 INITIAL TESTING

This chapter presents an analysis of the results obtained from the Attitude Scale, the Social Distance Scale, and the Projective Picture Test administered before the start of the Activity Group Program.*

Analysis of variance is used as a test of the differences between the attitudes of the two races. Scheffé's Multiple Comparisons Test is employed as a significance test of the differences between boys' and girls' attitudes and between the treatment groups. Pearson Product-Moment correlations are used as a measure of the relationship between reading ability and racial attitudes as well as the relationship between age and racial attitudes.

THE ATTITUDE SCALE

In both the fourth- and fifth-grade analysis of variance (Appendix D), the Negro pupils have a significantly higher (.01 level) mean score than do the white pupils. More favorable attitudes toward the other race are indicated by higher scores on the Attitude Scale.

For both the fourth and fifth grades, Scheffé's Test (Appendix D) shows no significant differences between races in the same treatment group or between treatment groups within the same race. Also, within the same race, there are no significant differences between boys and girls in either the fourth or fifth grades. The fifth grade has no significant differences between Negro and white boys or between Negro and white girls. However, in the fourth grade there is a significant difference between Negro and white

_____

*See Appendix D for tables of means and standard deviations.

75

girls at the .05 level. There is no significant
difference between fourth-grade Negro and white boys.

THE SOCIAL DISTANCE SCALE

In the fourth-grade analysis of variance (Appendix D), Negro pupils have a significantly higher
mean score (.05 level) than do the white pupils.
The fifth-grade Negro pupils (Appendix D) also have
a significantly higher mean score, but at the .01
level. More favorable attitudes toward the other
race are indicated by higher scores on the Social
Distance Scale.

For the fourth and fifth grades, Scheffé's Test
(Appendix D) shows no significant differences between
races in the same treatment group or between treatment groups within the same race. Neither the fourth
nor fifth grades has any significant differences
between boys and girls of the same race. The fourth
grade has no significant differences between Negro
and white boys or between Negro and white girls. The
fifth-grade Negro boys are significantly higher, .01
level, than are the white boys. The difference
between fifth-grade Negro and white girls is not
significant at the .05 level.

THE PROJECTIVE PICTURE TEST

For both fourth and fifth grades, the analysis
of variance (Appendix D) shows a significant difference, .01 level, between Negro and white pupils.
The significant difference means that the Negro
pupils have a more favorable attitude than do the
white pupils toward the other race.

Scheffé's Test (Appendix D) shows a significant
difference (.01 level) between Negro and white J-J
groups in both fourth and fifth grades. Also, in
the fourth grade a significant difference is found,
.05 level, between Negro and white J-S groups. All
significant differences indicate a more favorable
attitude of Negro pupils toward white pupils with a
corresponding less favorable attitude of white pupils
toward Negro pupils. Within each race, neither grade
has significant differences between treatment groups.
For both grades, there are no significant differences
between boys and girls of the same race. In both

grades, the Negro boys compared to white boys, and the Negro girls compared to white girls, have significantly higher mean scores (.01 level).

CORRELATIONS OF THE PRE-SCORES OF THE ATTITUDE MEASURES WITH READING AND AGE*

No significant relationships between reading ability and the pre-scores of the attitude measures are found for fourth-grade white, fifth-grade white, or fifth-grade Negro pupils. There is a significant positive correlation at the .01 level between both reading measures and the pre-scores of the Attitude Scale and the Social Distance Scale for fourth-grade Negro pupils. The fourth-grade Negro group shows a significant positive relationship (.05 level) between one test of reading ability, Reading, and the pre-scores of the Projective Picture Test.

There are no significant correlations between age and the pre-scores of the attitude measures for fourth-grade Negro, fifth-grade white, or fifth-grade Negro pupils. There is a significant positive relationship (.05 level) between age and the pre-scores of the Attitude Scale for fourth-grade white pupils.

INTERCORRELATIONS OF THE PRE-SCORES OF THE ATTITUDE MEASURES**

At the .01 level significant positive correlations are found in both fourth and fifth grades for the following: Attitude Scale vs. Social Distance Scale; Attitude Scale vs. Projective Picture Test; and Social Distance Scale vs. Projective Picture Test.

---

*See Appendix E for correlation tables.

**See Appendix E for correlation tables.

8

This chapter presents an analysis of the change results of the samples of Negro and white pupils obtained from the Attitude Scale, the Social Distance Scale, and the Projective Picture Test administered before and after the Activity Group Program.* Scheffé's Multiple Comparisons Test is used as a test of significance of the hypothesized differences in attitude change between the different treatment groups.

An additional analysis is done for the Attitude Scale scores. Using Word Knowledge and pre-test scores as concomitant variables and post-test scores as the dependent variable, multiple analyses of covariance are done for fourth- and fifth-grade Negro and white groups.

THE ATTITUDE SCALE

In the fourth grade, the Negro sample shows a decrease in mean score from pre- to post-tests, whereas the white mean remains fairly stable. On the Attitude Scale a negative change score indicates a change in racial attitude toward a less favorable direction. A positive change score indicates a change in racial attitude toward a more favorable direction. The Negro mean scores in the pre- and post-tests are higher than the white means, but there is greater variability in the white pupils with the most extreme changes in scores occurring among white pupils.

An analysis of variance, as given in Appendix G, based on the change from pre- to post-Attitude

----

*Tables 6-19 in this chapter. See Appendix F for tables of means and standard deviations.

Scale scores, indicates no significant difference between the changes in racial attitudes of fourth-grade Negro and white pupils.

In the fifth grade, the Negro sample has a slight decrease in mean score from pre- to post-tests, whereas for the white sample there is a slight increase.

An analysis of variance, as given in Appendix G, based on the change from pre- to post-Attitude Scale scores, indicates a significant difference between the changes in racial attitudes of fifth-grade Negro and white pupils at the .05 level.

THE SOCIAL DISTANCE SCALE

In the fourth grade, the Negro sample shows a slight decrease in mean score from pre- to post-tests, whereas for the white sample there is a slight increase. On the Social Distance Scale a negative change score indicates a change in racial attitude toward a less favorable direction. A positive change score indicates a change in racial attitude toward a more favorable direction.

The analysis of variance, as given in Appendix G, based on the changes from pre- to post-Social Distance Scale scores, indicates no significant differance between the changes in racial attitudes of fourth-grade Negro and white pupils.

In the fifth grade, Negro pupils show a slight decrease in mean score from pre- to post-tests, whereas for the white pupils there is a small increase.

An analysis of variance, as given in Appendix G, based on the change from pre- to post-Social Distance Scale scores, shows a significant difference between the changes in racial attitudes of Negro and white pupils at the .01 level.

THE PROJECTIVE PICTURE TEST

In the fourth grade, the Negro sample shows a decrease in positive mean score from pre- to post-tests, whereas the white mean becomes more negative. On the Projective Picture Test a negative change score indicates a change in racial attitude toward a less favorable direction. A positive change score indicates a change in racial attitude toward a more favorable direction.

An analysis of variance, as given in Appendix G, based on the change from pre- to post-Projective Picture Test scores, indicates no significant difference between the changes in racial attitudes of fourth-grade Negro and white pupils.

In the fifth grade, the Negro sample shows an increase in mean score from pre- to post-tests, whereas the white mean becomes more negative.

Results of an analysis of variance, as given in Appendix G, based on change from pre- to post-Projective Picture Test scores, show no significant difference between the changes in racial attitudes of fifth-grade Negro and white pupils.

CORRELATIONS OF THE CHANGE SCORES OF THE ATTITUDE
MEASURES WITH READING AND AGE*

The correlations are based on the total Negro and white samples and do not reflect differences in experimental treatments. No significant correlations between reading ability and change scores on the Attitude Scale and the Social Distance Scale are found for fourth-grade Negro, fourth-grade white, and fifth-grade white pupils. There is a significant positive correlation between both reading measures and the change scores of the Attitude Scale for fifth-grade Negro pupils. The fourth- and fifth-grade white groups show significant correlations, positive for the fourth and negative for the fifth, between one test of reading and the change scores of the Projective Picture Test.

There are no significant correlations between age and the change scores of the attitude measures for fourth-grade Negro, fourth-grade white, and fifth-grade white pupils. Fifth-grade Negro pupils show a significant negative correlation between age and the change scores of the Attitude Scale. On the Projective Picture Test, the fifth-grade Negro

---

*See Appendix E for correlation tables.

pupils have a significant positive correlation between
age and change scores.

INTERCORRELATIONS OF THE CHANGE SCORES
OF THE ATTITUDE MEASURES*

In the fourth and fifth grades, the only significant correlation is that of the Attitude Scale
with the Social Distance Scale for fifth-grade pupils
with a highly significant positive correlation of
.545.

TEST OF HYPOTHESES

Interracial Contact
vs. No Contact**

The first hypothesis predicts that significantly
greater positive change in racial attitudes will be
found in pupils who experience interracial contact
in the Activity Group Program than in those who experience no such interracial contact.

As seen in Tables 6 and 7, no significant differences are found between mean change Attitude
Scale, Social Distance Scale, or Projective Picture
Test scores of the interracial contact groups and
the no-contact group for either Negro or white
fourth-grade pupils.

As given in Tables 8 and 9 for fifth-grade Negro
or white pupils, none of the differences between
the mean change Attitude Scale, Social Distance
Scale or Projective Picture Test scores of the interracial contact groups and the no-contact group are
significant.

Therefore, Hypothesis 1, which concerns differences between interracial contact and no contact,
is not supported for fourth-grade Negro, fourth-
grade white, fifth-grade Negro or fifth-grade white
pupils on the Attitude Scale, the Social Distance
Scale, or the Projective Picture Test at the .05

---

*See Appendix E for correlation tables.

**See Tables 6-9 in this section.

TABLE 6

Scheffé's Multiple Comparisons Test of Hypothesis 1 for
Fourth-Grade Negro Pupils' Attitude Change Measures

Group Comparisons	Attitude Scale Absolute Difference in Means	Signif- icance Level	Social Distance Scale Absolute Difference in Means	Signif- icance Level	Projective Picture Test Absolute Difference in Means	Signif- icance Level
J-J vs. S-S	2.11	ns	.82	ns	1.28	ns
J-S vs. S-S	2.02	ns	1.12	ns	2.07	ns
S-J vs. S-S	.80	ns	5.26	ns	.19	ns
Msw	17.30		156.36		16.06	

82

TABLE 7

Scheffé's Multiple Comparisons Test of Hypothesis 1 for
Fourth-Grade White Pupils' Attitude Change Measures

Group Comparisons	Attitude Scale Absolute Difference in Means	Significance Level	Social Distance Scale Absolute Difference in Means	Significance Level	Projective Picture Test Absolute Difference in Means	Significance Level
J-J vs. S-S	3.21	ns	1.50	ns	2.48	ns
J-S vs. S-S	1.19	ns	1.45	ns	1.59	ns
S-J vs. S-S	1.19	ns	6.17	ns	.11	ns
Msw	21.09		126.64		10.12	

TABLE 8

Scheffé's Multiple Comparisons Test of Hypothesis 1 for
Fifth-Grade Negro Pupils' Attitude Change Measures

Group Comparisons	Attitude Scale Absolute Difference in Means	Significance Level	Social Distance Scale Absolute Difference in Means	Significance Level	Projective Picture Test Absolute Difference in Means	Significance Level
J-J vs. S-S	2.36	ns	5.36	ns	1.00	ns
J-S vs. S-S	2.94	ns	13.75	ns	.95	ns
S-J vs. S-S	2.53	ns	11.64	ns	.05	ns
Msw	9.96		182.11		13.17	

TABLE 9

Scheffé's Multiple Comparisons Test of Hypothesis 1 for
Fifth-Grade White Pupils' Attitude Change Measures

Group Comparisons	Attitude Scale Absolute Difference in Means	Signif- icance Level	Social Distance Scale Absolute Difference in Means	Signif- icance Level	Projective Picture Test Absolute Difference in Means	Signif- icance Level
J-J vs. S-S	.73	ns	4.95	ns	1.03	ns
J-S vs. S-S	.83	ns	3.93	ns	1.60	ns
S-J vs. S-S	3.45	ns	2.15	ns	.63	ns
Msw	11.30		115.92		13.94	

level.   There are no significant differences in the
change of racial attitudes of fourth- or fifth-grade
Negro or white pupils in the Activity Group Program
who experience interracial contact compared to those
pupils who do not.

Interracial Field Trip Contact vs.
Interracial Discussion Contact*

The second hypothesis predicts that among participants of the Activity Group Program significantly
greater positive changes in racial attitudes would
be found in pupils who experience interracial trip
contact than in those who experience interracial
discussion contact.

As given in Tables 10 and 11, no significant
differences are found between mean change Attitude
Scale, Social Distance Scale, or Projective Picture
Test scores of the interracial trip contact group
and the interracial discussion contact group for
either Negro or white fourth-grade pupils.

As seen in Tables 12 and 13 for fifth-grade
Negro or white pupils, none of the differences between
the mean change Attitude Scale, Social Distance Scale,
or Projective Picture Test scores of the interracial
trip contact group and the interracial discussion
contact group are significant.

Therefore, Hypothesis 2, which concerns field
trip contact and discussion contact, is not supported
for fourth-grade Negro, fourth-grade white, fifth-
grade Negro, or fifth-grade white pupils on the
Attitude Scale, the Social Distance Scale, or the
Projective Picture Test at the .05 level.   There are
no significant differences in the change of racial
attitudes of fourth- or fifth-grade Negro or white
pupils in the Activity Group Program who experience
interracial trip contact compared to those who experience discussion contact.

---

*See Tables 10-13 in this section.

TABLE 10

Scheffé's Multiple Comparisons Test of Hypothesis 2 for
Fourth-Grade Negro Pupils' Attitude Change Measures

Group Comparisons	Attitude Scale Absolute Difference in Means	Signif-icance Level	Social Distance Scale Absolute Difference in Means	Signif-icance Level	Projective Picture Test Absolute Difference in Means	Signif-icance Level
J-S vs. S-J	1.22	ns	6.38	ns	1.88	ns
Msw	17.30		156.36		16.06	

TABLE 11

Scheffé's Multiple Comparisons Test of Hypothesis 2 for
Fourth-Grade White Pupils' Attitude Change Measures

Group Comparisons	Attitude Scale Absolute Difference in Means	Signif-icance Level	Social Distance Scale Absolute Difference in Means	Signif-icance Level	Projective Picture Test Absolute Difference in Means	Signif-icance Level
J-S vs. S-J	0	ns	7.62	ns	1.48	ns
Msw	21.09		126.64		10.12	

TABLE 12

Scheffé's Multiple Comparisons Test of Hypothesis 2 for
Fifth-Grade Negro Pupils' Attitude Change Measures

Group Comparisons	Attitude Scale Absolute Difference in Means	Signif-icance Level	Social Distance Scale Absolute Difference in Means	Signif-icance Level	Projective Picture Test Absolute Difference in Means	Signif-icance Level
J-S vs. S-J	.41	ns	2.11	ns	.90	ns
Msw	9.96		182.11		13.17	

TABLE 13

Scheffé's Multiple Comparisons Test of Hypothesis 2 for
Fifth-Grade White Pupils' Attitude Change Measures

Group Comparisons	Attitude Scale Absolute Difference in Means	Signif-icance Level	Social Distance Scale Absolute Difference in Means	Signif-icance Level	Projective Picture Test Absolute Difference in Means	Signif-icance Level
J-S vs. S-J	.62	ns	1.78	ns	.97	ns
Msw	11.30		115.92		13.94	

Summation of Interracial Contact vs.
Interracial Trip or Interracial
Discussion Contact*

The third hypothesis predicts that among participants of the Activity Group Program significantly
greater positive changes in racial attitudes would
be found in pupils who experience both interracial
trip contact and discussion contact than in those
who experience only one or the other.

As given in Tables 14 and 15, no significant
differences are found between mean change Attitude
Scale, Social Distance Scale, or Projective Picture
Test scores of the interracial trip and discussion
contact group, and the interracial trip or interracial discussion contact groups for either Negro
or white fourth-grade pupils.

As seen in Tables 16 and 17 for the fifth grade,
significant differences are found between the mean
change Attitude Scale score of the interracial trip
and discussion contact group and each of the scores
of the interracial trip contact group and the interracial discussion contact group for Negro pupils at
the .01 level.

Therefore, Hypothesis 3, which involves the
combined effects of interracial trip contact and
discussion contact compared to one or the other,
is not supported for fourth-grade Negro, fourth-
grade white, fifth-grade Negro, or fifth-grade
white pupils on the Social Distance Scale or the
Projective Picture Test at the .05 level. There
also is no support for Hypothesis 3 for fourth-
grade Negro, fourth-grade white, or fifth-grade
white pupils on the Attitude Scale. There are no
significant differences in the change of racial
attitudes of fourth-grade Negro, fourth-grade white,
or fifth-grade white pupils in the Activity Group
Program who experience interracial trip contact
and interracial discussion contact compared to
those pupils who experience only one or the other.
Hypothesis 3 is sustained for fifth-grade Negro
pupils on the Attitude Scale at the .01 level. The
fifth-grade Negro pupils who experience interracial

---

*See Tables 14-17 in this section.

TABLE 14

Scheffé's Multiple Comparisons Test of Hypothesis 3 for
Fourth-Grade Negro Pupils' Attitude Change Measures

Group Comparisons	Attitude Scale Absolute Difference in Means	Significance Level	Social Distance Scale Absolute Difference in Means	Significance Level	Projective Picture Test Absolute Difference in Means	Significance Level
J-J vs. J-S	.09	ns	1.94	ns	.79	ns
J-J vs. S-J	1.31	ns	4.44	ns	1.09	ns
Msw	17.30		156.36		16.06	

TABLE 15

Scheffé's Multiple Comparisons Test of Hypothesis 3 for
Fourth-Grade White Pupils' Attitude Change Measures

Group Comparisons	Attitude Scale Absolute Difference in Means	Signif- icance Level	Social Distance Scale Absolute Difference in Means	Signif- icance Level	Projective Picture Test Absolute Difference in Means	Signif- icance Level
J-J vs. J-S	2.02	ns	2.95	ns	.89	ns
J-J vs. S-J	2.02	ns	4.67	ns	2.37	ns
Msw	21.09		126.64		10.12	

TABLE 16

Scheffé's Multiple Comparisons Test of Hypothesis 3 for
Fifth-Grade Negro Pupils' Attitude Change Measures

Group Comparisons	Attitude Scale Absolute Difference in Means	Signif-icance Level	Social Distance Scale Absolute Difference in Means	Signif-icance Level	Projective Picture Test Absolute Difference in Means	Signif-icance Level
J-J vs. J-S	5.30	.01	8.39	ns	.05	ns
J-J vs. S-J	4.89	.01	6.28	ns	.95	ns
Msw	9.96		182.11		13.17	

TABLE 17

Scheffé's Multiple Comparisons Test of Hypothesis 3 for
Fifth-Grade White Pupils' Attitude Change Measures

Group Comparisons	Attitude Scale Absolute Difference in Means	Signif- icance Level	Social Distance Scale Absolute Difference in Means	Signif- icance Level	Projective Picture Test Absolute Difference in Means	Signif- icance Level
J-J vs. J-S	.10	ns	1.02	ns	.57	ns
J-J vs. S-J	2.72	ns	2.80	ns	.40	ns
Msw	11.30		115.92		13.94	

trip contact and discussion contact have a significantly more positive change in racial attitude than
the fifth-grade Negro pupils who experience interracial trip or discussion contact.

In summary, none of the hypotheses are supported
in the fourth-grade for Negro or white pupils. In
the fifth-grade only Hypothesis 3 receives support
for fifth-grade Negro pupils on the Attitude Scale.

Further Analysis of Findings*

There is a significant difference found in the
Attitude Scale change scores of fifth-grade Negro
pupils. Specifically, significant differences are
found between the mean change score of the interracial trip and discussion contact group (J-J) and
each of the scores of the interracial trip contact
group (J-S) and the interracial discussion contact
group (S-J). Therefore, since it is felt that the
significant differences found could be due to differences in reading ability and initial attitudes,
multiple analyses of variance are done. Two concomitant measures are used: Word Knowledge and
Attitude Scale Pre Test Scores. Word Knowledge is
used as a measure of reading ability. Since both
reading tests are highly correlated, it is not considered necessary to use both reading measures. The
multiple analyses of covariance are done for fourth-
and fifth-grade Negro and white groups even though
the significant difference is found only in the fifth-
grade Negro group.

As given in Table 18, the F's of 2.95 for fifth-
grade Negro pupils and 2.85 for fifth-grade white
pupils are significant at the .05 level. The adjusted post means have been changed considerably from
the original post means for both groups (Table 19).

To test the hypothesized differences among the
adjusted post means, Scheffé's Multiple Comparisons
Test is used. For fifth-grade Negro pupils using
the change scores, J-J vs. J-S and J-J vs. S-J are
significant at the .01 level. However, using the
adjusted post means, J-J vs. J-S has a Scheffé .95
confidence interval of -.01, 7.83 which is not quite

---

*See Tables 18 and 19 in this section.

TABLE 18

Multiple Analysis of Covariance of Attitude
Scale Post-Scores with Word Knowledge
and Attitude Scale Pre-Scores as
Covariates for Fourth- and
Fifth-Grade Negro and
White Pupils

Group	Source	df	MS	F
4th-Grade Negro	Treatments	3	.06	.004
	Error	60	14.14	
4th-Grade White	Treatments	3	23.32	1.59
	Error	56	14.67	
5th-Grade Negro	Treatments	3	27.90	2.95*
	Error	49	9.45	
5th-Grade White	Treatments	3	32.29	2.85*
	Error	54	11.32	

*Significant at .05 level

TABLE 19

Attitude Scale Post- and Adjusted Post-Means
According to Treatment Groups of Fourth-
and Fifth-Grade Negro and
White Pupils

Group	Treatment	Post Mean	Adjusted Post Mean
4th-Grade Negro	J-J	10.00	9.32
	J-S	9.81	9.12
	S-J	8.71	9.14
	S-S	7.93	9.13
4th-Grade White	J-J	9.24	9.10
	J-S	7.92	7.43
	S-J	4.12	5.42
	S-S	7.67	7.50
5th-Grade Negro	J-J	11.72	12.05
	J-S	8.81	8.14
	S-J	10.89	8.94
	S-S	8.75	10.62
5th-Grade White	J-J	8.38	8.53
	J-S	9.29	8.75
	S-J	11.77	11.34
	S-S	6.83	7.66

significant. At the .90 level, the confidence interval of .42, 7.40 is significant. J-J vs. S-J is not
significant at the .95 or .90 levels. For fifth-
grade white pupils, there are no significant differences between any of the adjusted means at the
.95 or .90 levels.

SUMMARY OF FINDINGS

Scheffé's Multiple Comparisons Test, using
Attitude Scale change scores, shows significant differences only among the treatment groups of the fifth-
grade Negro pupils. For both the white and Negro
pupils of the fifth grade, there are significant F's
(at the .05 level) in the multiple analysis of covariance of the Attitude Scale post-scores with Word
Knowledge and Attitude Scale pre-scores as the concomitant variables. However, using Scheffé's Multiple Comparisons Test, there are no significant differences (at .95 level) among the treatment groups
of either the Negro or white pupils. Therefore, the
previous significant differences with change scores
are not found using the adjusted post test scores of
the multiple analysis of covariance.

CHAPTER **9** SUPPLEMENTARY RESULTS*

The data presented in this chapter explore the relationship between aspects of the Activity Group Experience and pupils' attitude change. Items of the Trip Rating Sheet and observational material describing teacher behavior are analyzed to evaluate the relevance of Cook's dimensions of interracial contact--acquaintance potential, relative status of the participants, and the social norm toward contact--to attitude change.

The acquaintance potential in the interracial partner contact--the degree to which pupils could communicate, get acquainted, and gain satisfaction in the partner relationship--is assessed from the pupils' expressed feelings about continued assignment to the same partners (Item 2, Trip Rating Sheet). The relative status of the pupil partners is determined from the pupils' evaluations of their own ideas compared to those of their partners (Item 3, Trip Rating Sheet). The social norm toward interracial contact is evaluated from the observational material describing teacher behavior. Therefore, the data pertinent to each of Cook's dimensions are analyzed and compared to the racial attitude change results of the present study.

Further supplementary data are presented to evaluate the relationship of other aspects of the Activity Group Program to attitude change. The following additional data are analyzed and compared to the racial attitude change results: (1) pupils' perceptions of the skill of teachers and discussion leaders (Items 1 and 2, Teacher-Discussion Leader Rating Sheet); (2) pupils' attitudes toward the trips in general (Item 1, Trip Rating Sheet); and

---

*Tables 20-33 in this chapter.

98

(3) pupils' previously existing attitudes toward their own classes (My Teacher, Classroom Life, and How This Class Thinks).

The data are organized in three sections: (1) partner relationship; (2) trip properties (including the observations of teacher behavior and the pupils' perceptions of teachers and discussion leaders; and (3) characteristics of classroom experience.

PARTNER RELATIONSHIP

Pupil Perception of Partner

Item 2 of the Trip Rating Sheet refers to the pupils' perceptions of their partners.* Based on the cumulative score for the three trips, the pupils are divided into three categories according to feeling about assignment to the same partners on future trips: (1) wanting same partner; (2) neutral; and (3) not wanting same partner. Since cumulative scores from the three trips can reflect either consistency or in-consistency of response from trip to trip, assignment to a category is based on a minimum of two responses in the same category. Change scores on the Attitude Scale are also divided into three categories: (1) positive attitude change; (2) no change; and (3) negative attitude change.

As given in Table 20 of the 127 interracial partners who have a positive change in attitude, 106 show a preference for the same partners for future trips. Only 52 of the 108 interracial partners with a negative change in attitude express a preference for the same partners. Preference for the partner seems to be closely related to attitude change.

Pupil Evaluations of Own Ideas
and Partner's Ideas

Item 3 of the Trip Rating Sheet refers to the pupil's judgment of the value of his own ideas com-pared to those of his partner.** Based on the cumu-lative score for the three trips, the subjects are

---

*See Table 20 in this section.

**See Table 21 in this section.

TABLE 20

Relationship Between Item 2 of Trip Rating Sheets I and II
and Attitude Scale Change Scores

		Attitude Scale Change														
		Fourth-Grade						Fifth-Grade								
		White			Negro			White			Negro					
Group	Perception of Partner	+	0	-	+	0	-	+	0	-	+	0	-
Trip Rating Sheet I Interracial Partners													
J-J + J-S	Want	16	1	6	12	7	10	13	1	4	11	3	7
	Neutral	3	0	2	0	0	3	0	3	2	1	0	5
	Not Want	0	0	6	1	0	2	2	0	10	1	2	4
Trip Rating Sheet II Interracial Partners													
J-J + S-J	Want	15	2	5	13	7	11	14	1	5	12	3	4
	Neutral	4	0	3	2	0	1	1	3	1	1	0	1
	Not Want	3	0	5	0	0	2	1	2	6	1	2	3
Trip Rating Sheet I Same Race Partners													
S-J + S-S	Want	8	3	8	10	5	5	10	1	5	6	0	5
	Neutral	0	1	2	0	3	4	1	1	1	0	3	1
	Not Want	2	0	4	2	1	1	0	2	4	1	0	5
Trip Rating Sheet II Same Race Partners													
J-S + S-S	Want	6	3	8	5	7	4	7	1	5	4	1	10
	Neutral	0	0	2	0	0	4	1	0	2	1	1	2
	Not Want	1	0	5	5	2	3	2	1	7	1	1	7

TABLE 21

Relationship between Item 3 of Trip Rating Sheets I and II and Attitude Scale Change Scores

	Perception of Partner	Attitude Scale Change											
		Fourth-Grade						Fifth-Grade					
		White			Negro			White			Negro		
Group	Status	+	0	-	+	0	-	+	0	-	+	0	-
Trip Rating Sheet I Interracial Partners													
J-J + J-S	Equal	17	0	8	13	7	11	14	2	5	13	3	8
	Unequal	2	1	6	0	0	4	1	2	11	0	2	8
Trip Rating Sheet II Interracial Partners													
J-J + S-J	Equal	20	1	8	14	6	7	16	3	4	13	5	5
	Unequal	2	1	5	1	1	7	0	3	8	1	0	3
Trip Rating Sheet I Same Race Partners													
S-J + S-S	Equal	9	4	7	10	7	2	10	1	5	5	2	5
	Unequal	1	0	7	2	2	8	1	3	5	2	1	6
Trip Rating Sheet II Same Race Partners													
J-S + S-S	Equal	5	3	6	7	5	6	8	1	7	5	2	11
	Unequal	2	0	9	3	4	5	2	1	7	1	1	8

divided into two categories: (1) those judging own ideas and partner's ideas to be equal in value; and (2) those judging own ideas and partner's ideas to be unequal in value. Since cumulative scores from the three trips can reflect either consistency or inconsistency of response from trip to trip, assignment to a category is based on a minimum of two responses in the same category. Change scores on the Attitude Scale are also divided into three categories: (1) positive attitude change; (2) no change; and (3) negative attitude change.

As given in Table 21, only seven of the 127 interracial partners whose attitudes changed positively indicated that their own ideas and those of their partners are unequal in value. However, about half (52) of the 108 interracial partners who show a negative change of attitude are found in the unequal category. Perception of equality between partners seems to be closely related to attitude change.

TRIP PROPERTIES

Pupil Perception of
Trip Experience

Item 1 of the Trip Rating Sheet refers to the pupils' feelings about the trip.* Based on the cumulative score for the three trips, the pupils are divided into three categories: (1) those liking the trip; (2) those neutral about the trip; and (3) those disliking the trip. Since cumulative scores from the three trips can reflect either consistency or inconsistency of response from trip to trip, assignment to a category is based on a minimum of two responses in the same category. Change scores on the Attitude Scale are also divided into three categories: (1) positive attitude change; (2) no change; and (3) negative attitude change.

As given in Table 22, five of the 127 interracial partners whose attitudes change positively indicate a dislike for the trip. Only eight of the 108 interracial partners whose attitudes change negatively show a dislike for the trip. Thus the attitude

---

*See Table 22 in this section.

TABLE 22

Relationship Between Item 1 of Trip Rating Sheets I and II
and Attitude Scale Change Scores

		Attitude Scale Change											
		Fourth-Grade						Fifth-Grade					
		White			Negro			White			Negro		
Group	Perception of Trip	+	0	-	+	0	-	+	0	-	+	0	-
Trip Rating Sheet I Interracial Partners													
J-J + J-S	Like	17	0	11	13	7	12	11	2	8	12	4	10
	Neutral	2	1	1	0	0	3	2	1	5	1	1	5
	Dislike	0	0	2	0	0	0	2	1	3	0	0	1
Trip Rating Sheet II Interracial Partners													
J-J + S-J	Like	20	1	10	13	6	13	15	4	6	13	5	7
	Neutral	1	1	2	2	1	1	0	2	5	0	0	1
	Dislike	1	0	1	0	0	0	1	0	1	1	0	0
Trip Rating Sheet I Same Race Partners													
S-J + S-S	Like	10	3	11	12	7	6	10	4	5	6	3	9
	Neutral	0	1	3	0	0	3	1	0	5	0	0	2
	Dislike	0	0	0	0	2	1	0	0	0	1	0	0
Trip Rating Sheet II Same Race Partners													
J-S + S-S	Like	7	1	14	10	6	9	6	2	6	5	2	13
	Neutral	0	2	1	0	1	1	2	0	6	0	0	6
	Dislike	0	0	0	0	2	1	2	0	2	1	1	0

103

toward the trip, unlike the attitude toward the partner, is not differentially related to racial attitude change.

Pupil Perception of Teacher

Item 1 of the Teacher-Discussion Leader Rating Sheet refers to the pupils' perceptions about the teachers' behavior on the trip.* Based on the cumulative score for the three trips, the subjects are divided into two categories: (1) those who think the teacher did a good job; and (2) those who think the teacher did an average or bad job. Since cumulative scores from the three trips can reflect either consistency or inconsistency of response from trip to trip, assignment to a category is based on a minimum of two responses in the same category. Change scores on the Attitude Scale are also divided into three categories: (1) positive attitude change; (2) no change; and (3) negative attitude change.

As given in Table 23, among those pupils who rate the teacher's job as good, there is almost equal frequency of positive attitude change (79 pupils) and negative attitude change (85 pupils). Likewise, of those pupils rating the teacher's job as average-bad, there is equal frequency between positive attitude change (21 pupils) and negative attitude change (21 pupils). There seems to be little relationship between attitude change and perception of teacher's skill on the trip.

Pupil Perception of Discussion Leader

Item 2 of the Teacher-Discussion Leader Rating Sheet refers to the pupils' perceptions about the discussion leaders' behavior on the trip.** Based on the cumulative score for the three trips, the subjects are divided into two categories: (1) those who think the discussion leader did a good job; and (2) those who think the discussion leader did an average or bad job. Since cumulative scores from the three trips can reflect either consistency or inconsistency of responses from trip to trip, assignment to a category is based on a minimum of two responses in the

---

*See Table 23 in this section.

**See Table 24 in this section.

TABLE 23

Relationship Between Item 1 of Teacher-Discussion Leader Rating Sheet and Attitude Scale Change Scores

Group	Perception of Teacher	Fourth-Grade White			Fourth-Grade Negro			Fifth-Grade White			Fifth-Grade Negro		
		+	0	-	+	0	-	+	0	-	+	0	-
J-J	Good Job	10	1	3	6	6	6	7	3	8	6	3	2
	Average-Bad	4	0	3	1	0	0	1	1	1	6	0	1
J-S	Good Job	5	0	6	4	1	9	6	0	5	0	2	11
	Average-Bad	0	0	2	2	0	0	1	0	2	1	0	2
S-J	Good Job	8	1	6	7	1	6	6	2	3	2	2	3
	Average-Bad	0	0	1	1	0	2	2	0	0	0	0	2
S-S	Good Job	2	3	7	4	6	2	2	2	3	4	1	5
	Average-Bad	0	0	0	0	2	0	1	0	4	1	0	1
Totals	Good Job	25	5	22	21	14	23	21	7	19	12	8	21
	Average-Bad	4	0	6	4	2	2	5	1	7	8	0	6

Attitude Scale Change

105

TABLE 24

Relationship Between Item 2 of Teacher-Discussion Leader Rating Sheet and Attitude Scale Change Scores

Group	Perception of Discussion Leader	Fourth-Grade White			Fourth-Grade Negro			Fifth-Grade White			Fifth-Grade Negro		
		+	0	−	+	0	−	+	0	−	+	0	−
J-J	Good Job	9	0	2	4	6	6	4	3	5	10	3	2
	Average-Bad	5	1	4	3	0	0	4	1	4	2	0	1
J-S	Good Job	3	0	7	2	1	6	4	0	4	1	0	9
	Average-Bad	2	0	1	4	0	3	3	0	3	0	2	4
S-J	Good Job	4	1	4	5	1	4	8	1	1	2	2	5
	Average-Bad	4	0	3	3	0	4	0	1	2	0	0	0
S-S	Good Job	1	1	4	3	5	2	1	2	3	5	1	6
	Average-Bad	1	2	3	1	3	0	2	0	4	0	0	0
Totals	Good Job	17	2	17	14	13	18	17	6	13	18	6	22
	Average-Bad	12	3	11	11	3	7	9	2	13	2	2	5

Attitude Scale Change

same category. Change scores on the Attitude Scale
are divided into three categories: (1) positive
attitude change; (2) no change; and (3) negative
attitude change.

As shown in Table 24, among those pupils who
rate the discussion leader's job as good, 66 show
a positive attitude change, whereas 70 have a negative attitude change. Likewise, of those pupils
rating the discussion leader's job as average-bad,
34 have a positive attitude change and 36 show a
negative attitude change. There seems to be little
relationship between attitude change and perception
of discussion leader's skill.

Ratings of Teacher Behavior

Using observation reports (Appendix D), two
judges rate teacher behavior in regard to support
of friendly interracial contact.* The behavior of
the four teachers in each of the interracial treatment groups is rated. Since the S-S groups did not
have interracial contact, teachers in those groups
are not evaluated. Based on the three trips, the
judges separated the teacher behavior into two
categories: (1) behavior definitely supportive of
friendly interracial contact; and (2) other behavior
including somewhat supportive, neutral, and not
supportive of friendly interracial contact. Change
scores of the Attitude Scale are also divided into
three categories: (1) positive attitude change; (2)
no change; and (3) negative attitude change. Since
the two judges are in agreement in evaluating teacher
behavior, only one rating for each teacher is given.

As seen in Table 25, the behavior of the fifth-
grade teacher in the Negro J-J group is judged as
definitely supportive of friendly interracial contact.
The remaining 11 teachers are rated as less than
definitely supportive. In the classes of the 11
teachers, 72 pupils have a positive change of attitude and 81 show a negative change of attitude. In
the one class with the definitely supportive teacher,
12 pupils show a positive attitude change and three
have a negative attitude change. There seems to be
a relationship between teacher behavior and racial
attitude change.

---

*See Table 25 in this section.

TABLE 25

Relationship Between Judges' Ratings of Teacher Behavior
and Attitude Scale Change Scores

			Attitude Scale Change											
			Fourth-Grade						Fifth-Grade					
			White			Negro			White			Negro		
Group	Teacher Behavior	N	+	0	-	+	0	-	+	0	-	+	0	-
J-J	Definitely Supportive	1										12	3	3
	Other	3	14	1	6	7	6	6	8	4	9			13
J-S	Definitely Supportive	0												
	Other	4	5	0	8	6	1	9	7	0	7	1	2	
S-J	Definitely Supportive	0												
	Other	4	8	1	7	8	1	8	6	2	3	2	2	5
Totals	Definitely Supportive	1										12	3	3
	Other	11	27	2	21	21	8	23	21	6	19	3	4	18

CHARACTERISTICS OF CLASSROOM EXPERIENCE

Pupil Perception of Teacher

Items 8, 9, and 10 of My Teacher refer to the
pupils' satisfaction with teacher behavior in the
following areas: Item 8, friendliness; Item 9,
understanding of pupils' feelings; and Item 10, helping pupils to understand each other.* The subjects
are divided into two categories: (1) those wanting
the teacher to remain the same; and (2) those wanting
the teacher to change. Change scores on the Attitude
Scale are divided into three categories: (1) positive
attitude change; (2) no change; and (3) negative attitude change.

As seen in Table 26, of those pupils who want
the teacher to remain the same in friendliness, 43
show a positive attitude change and 40 have a negative attitude change. Likewise, among those pupils
who want a change in the teacher, 57 show a positive
attitude change and 66 have a negative attitude
change.

As seen in Table 27, of those pupils who want
the teacher to remain the same in understanding, 31
show a positive attitude change and 33 have a negative attitude change. Likewise, among those pupils
who want a change in the teacher, 69 show a positive
change of attitude and 73 have a negative attitude
change.

As seen in Table 28, of those pupils who want
the teacher to remain the same in helping pupils
understand each other, 32 show a positive attitude
change and 34 have a negative attitude change. Among
pupils who want a change, 65 have a positive attitude
change and 72 show a negative attitude change. In
summary, the pupils' perception of the teacher's
classroom behavior seems unrelated to racial attitude
change.

Pupil Perception of Classroom Life

Items A, D, and F of Classroom Life refer to
the pupils' perceptions of classroom life in the

---

*See Tables 26, 27, and 28 in this section.

TABLE 26

Relationship Between Item 8 of My Teacher and
Attitude Scale Change Scores

		Attitude Scale Change										
		Fourth-Grade						Fifth-Grade					
		White			Negro			White			Negro		
Group	Perception of Teacher Friendliness	+	0	-	+	0	-	+	0	-	+	0	-
J-J	Same	10	1	4	4	4	3	4	2	6	2	2	1
	Change	4	0	2	3	2	3	4	2	3	10	1	2
J-S	Same	3	0	5	3	1	3	3	0	2	1	0	3
	Change	2	0	3	3	0	6	4	0	5	0	2	10
S-J	Same	2	0	0	1	0	2	4	1	1	1	1	2
	Change	6	1	7	7	1	6	4	1	2	1	1	3
S-S	Same	1	1	2	2	4	1	1	0	3	1	0	2
	Change	1	2	5	2	4	1	2	2	4	4	1	4
Totals	Same	16	2	11	10	9	9	12	3	12	5	3	8
	Change	13	3	17	15	7	16	14	5	14	15	5	19

110

TABLE 27

Relationship Between Item 9 of My Teacher and
Attitude Scale Change Scores

	Perception of Teacher Understanding	Attitude Scale Change											
		Fourth-Grade						Fifth-Grade					
		White			Negro			White			Negro		
Group		+	0	−	+	0	−	+	0	−	+	0	−
J-J	Same	8	1	0	4	5	2	0	2	3	2	1	1
	Change	6	0	6	3	1	4	8	2	6	10	2	2
J-S	Same	2	0	1	2	1	3	2	0	3	1	0	6
	Change	3	0	7	4	0	6	5	0	4	0	2	7
S-J	Same	1	0	2	2	1	1	2	1	0	1	1	2
	Change	7	1	5	6	0	7	6	1	3	1	1	3
S-S	Same	1	1	4	2	2	1	1	2	3	0	0	1
	Change	1	2	3	2	6	1	2	0	4	5	1	5
Totals	Same	12	2	7	10	9	7	5	5	9	4	2	10
	Change	17	3	21	15	7	18	21	3	17	16	6	17

111

TABLE 28

Relationship Between Item 10 of My Teacher and
Attitude Scale Change Scores

Perception of Teacher Help in Pupils Understanding Each Other	Attitude Scale Change											
	Fourth-Grade						Fifth-Grade					
	White			Negro			White			Negro		
Group	+	0	–	+	0	–	+	0	–	+	0	–
J–J Same	9	1	0	4	4	3	2	3	5	2	0	1
Change	5	0	6	3	2	3	6	1	4	10	3	2
J–S Same	3	0	2	2	1	4	2	0	3	1	0	4
Change	2	0	6	4	0	5	5	0	4	0	2	9
S–J Same	3	0	2	1	0	1	3	0	0	1	1	2
Change	5	1	5	7	1	7	5	2	3	1	1	3
S–S Same	1	1	3	1	3	1	0	1	1	0	0	2
Change	1	2	4	3	5	1	3	1	6	5	1	4
Totals Same	16	2	7	8	8	9	7	4	9	4	1	9
Change	13	3	21	17	8	16	19	4	17	16	7	18

112

following areas: Item A, goodness of life in class
with the teacher; Item D, friendliness of pupils;
and Item F, level of work in class.*

For Item A the pupils are divided into two
categories: (1) those pupils judging life in class
as all good; and (2) those pupils judging life in
class as less than all good.   For Item D the pupils
are divided into the following two categories: (1)
those pupils judging classmates as friendly; and
(2) those pupils judging classmates as unfriendly.
For Item F the pupils are also divided into two
categories: (1) those pupils who work hard in class;
and (2) those pupils who are not working hard in
class.   Change scores on the Attitude Scale are divided into three categories: (1) positive attitude
change; (2) no change; and (3) negative attitude
change.

As seen in Table 29, of those pupils who rate
classroom life as all good, 45 show a positive attitude change and 49 have a negative attitude change.
Similarly, among those pupils who do not perceive
classroom life as all good, 55 have a positive attitude change and 57 show a negative attitude change.

As seen in Table 30, of those pupils who perceive the class as friendly, 61 have a positive
attitude change and 57 show a negative attitude
change.   Among those pupils who perceive the class
as unfriendly, 39 show a positive attitude change
and 49 have a negative attitude change.

As seen in Table 31, of those pupils who perceive themselves as working hard in class, there is
an equal frequency (65) of pupils with positive and
negative attitude change.   Of those pupils who perceive themselves as not working hard, 35 show a positive attitude change and 41 have a negative attitude
change.   In summary, the pupils' perception of classroom life seems unrelated to racial attitude change.

Pupil Perception of Class Attitudes

Items 4 and 5 of How This Class Thinks refer
to the pupil's estimate of the number of his classmates who like schoolwork (Item 4) and who view the

---

*See Tables 29, 30, and 31 in this section.

TABLE 29

Relationship Between Item A of Classroom Life and
Attitude Scale Change Scores

Group	Perception of Goodness of Classroom Life	Attitude Scale Change																						
		Fourth-Grade						Fifth-Grade																
		White			Negro			White			Negro													
		+	0	−	+	0	−	+	0	−	+	0	−											
J-J	All Good	6	0	3	3	4	3	3	0	1	6	1	1											
	Others	8	1	3	4	2	3	5	4	8	6	2	2											
J-S	All Good	4	0	3	3	0	3	0	0	2	1	2	6											
	Others	1	0	5	3	1	6	7	0	5	0	0	7											
S-J	All Good	6	1	6	3	1	2	2	0	2	0	1	3											
	Others	2	0	1	5	0	6	6	2	1	2	1	2											
S-S	All Good	1	2	6	3	5	2	1	1	2	3	1	4											
	Others	1	1	1	1	3	0	2	1	5	2	0	2											
Totals	All Good	17	3	18	12	10	10	6	1	7	10	5	14											
	Others	12	2	10	13	6	15	20	7	19	10	3	13											

TABLE 30

Relationship Between Item D of Classroom Life and
Attitude Scale Change Scores

	Perception of Friendliness of Pupils	Attitude Scale Change											
Group		Fourth-Grade						Fifth-Grade					
		White			Negro			White			Negro		
		+	0	−	+	0	−	+	0	−	+	0	−
J-J	Friendly	11	1	5	4	4	4	6	2	6	9	2	2
	Unfriendly	3	0	1	3	2	2	2	2	3	3	1	1
J-S	Friendly	5	0	4	3	0	4	4	0	2	1	2	6
	Unfriendly	0	0	4	3	1	5	3	0	5	0	0	7
S-J	Friendly	3	0	4	5	1	4	4	2	0	1	2	3
	Unfriendly	5	1	3	3	0	4	4	0	3	1	0	2
S-S	Friendly	1	3	6	1	4	1	1	0	2	2	0	4
	Unfriendly	1	0	1	3	4	1	2	2	5	3	1	2
Totals	Friendly	20	4	19	13	9	13	15	4	10	13	6	15
	Unfriendly	9	1	9	12	7	12	11	4	16	7	2	12

115

TABLE 31

Relationship Between Item F of Classroom Life and
Attitude Scale Change Scores

	Perception of Own Classroom Work	Attitude Scale Change											
		Fourth-Grade						Fifth-Grade					
		White			Negro			White			Negro		
Group		+	0	-	+	0	-	+	0	-	+	0	-
J-J	Hard	9	1	4	5	5	6	7	3	8	10	2	3
	Not Hard	5	0	2	2	1	0	1	1	1	2	1	0
J-S	Hard	4	0	5	4	1	4	4	0	6	1	2	5
	Not Hard	1	0	3	2	0	5	3	0	1	0	0	8
S-J	Hard	5	0	4	4	0	2	3	1	3	2	2	2
	Not Hard	3	1	3	4	1	6	5	1	0	0	0	3
S-S	Hard	0	2	6	2	5	1	2	0	1	3	0	5
	Not Hard	2	1	1	2	3	1	1	2	6	2	1	1
Totals	Hard	18	3	19	15	11	13	16	4	18	16	6	15
	Not Hard	11	2	9	10	5	12	10	4	8	4	2	12

116

teacher as understanding (Item 5).* For Item 4 the
pupils are divided into two categories: (1) those
pupils who perceive half or more of the class as
liking schoolwork; and (2) those pupils who perceive
some or few of the class as liking schoolwork. For
Item 5 the pupils are also divided into two categories: (1) those pupils who perceive half or more
of the class as feeling the teacher is understanding;
and (2) those pupils who perceive some or few of the
class as feeling the teacher is understanding. Change
scores on the Attitude Scale are divided into three
categories: (1) positive attitude change; (2) no
change; and (3) negative attitude change.

As seen in Table 32, among those pupils who perceive at least half of their classmates as liking
schoolwork, 55 show a positive attitude change and
58 have a negative attitude change. Similarly, of
those pupils who perceived some or few of their
classmates as liking schoolwork, 45 have a positive
attitude change and 48 show a negative attitude
change.

As seen in Table 33, among those pupils who
estimate that at least half of their classmates perceive the teacher as understanding, 71 have a positive attitude change and 74 show a negative attitude
change. Likewise, of those who estimate that only
some or few perceive the teacher as understanding,
29 show a positive attitude change and 32 have a
negative attitude change. In summary, the pupils'
perceptions of how their classmates view classwork
and the teacher seem unrelated to racial attitude
change.

SUMMARY

Supplementary results indicate that Cook's
three-dimension analysis of the interracial contact
situation--acquaintance potential, relative status
of the participants, and the social norm toward
interracial contact--are influential factors in
racial attitude change. Support for the influence
of Cook's dimensions are found in the data from the
Trip Rating Sheets and judgments of teacher behavior.

---

*See Tables 32 and 33 in this section.

TABLE 32

Relationship Between Item 4 of How This Class Thinks
and Attitude Scale Change Scores

Group	Estimate of Pupils who Like Schoolwork	Fourth-Grade White			Fourth-Grade Negro			Fifth-Grade White			Fifth-Grade Negro		
		+	0	-	+	0	-	+	0	-	+	0	-
J-J	Most-half	7	1	4	4	3	4	7	2	5	6	2	1
	Few-some	7	0	2	3	3	2	1	2	4	6	1	2
J-S	Most-half	2	0	4	4	0	6	1	0	1	1	2	6
	Few-some	3	0	4	2	1	3	6	0	6	0	0	7
S-J	Most-half	4	0	2	5	1	5	5	2	1	1	0	5
	Few-some	4	1	5	3	0	3	3	0	2	1	2	0
S-S	Most-half	1	3	3	1	7	2	2	0	4	4	0	5
	Few-some	1	0	4	3	1	0	1	2	3	1	1	1
Totals	Most-half	14	4	13	14	11	17	15	4	11	12	4	17
	Few-some	15	1	15	11	5	8	11	4	15	8	4	10

TABLE 33

Relationship Between Item 5 of How This Class Thinks
and Attitude Scale Change Scores

Group	Estimate of Pupils Who Think Teacher is Understanding	Attitude Scale Change																							
		Fourth-Grade						Fifth-Grade											
		White			Negro			White			Negro		
		+	0	−	+	0	−	+	0	−	+	0	−
J-J	Most-half	11	0	6	4	4	4	7	3	8	9	3	2
	Few-some	3	1	0	3	2	2	1	1	1	3	0	1
J-S	Most-half	2	0	6	5	1	7	5	0	5	1	2	8
	Few-some	3	0	2	1	0	2	2	0	2	0	0	5
S-J	Most-half	6	0	5	5	1	5	6	1	1	1	2	3
	Few-some	2	1	2	3	0	3	2	1	2	1	0	2
S-S	Most-half	2	1	5	3	4	2	3	1	3	1	0	4
	Few-some	0	2	2	1	4	0	0	1	4	4	1	2
Totals	Most-half	21	1	22	17	10	18	21	5	17	12	7	17
	Few-some	8	4	6	8	6	7	5	3	9	8	1	10

Pupils who express a desire for continued assignment to the same partner are more likely to have a positive racial attitude change. Similarly, pupils who perceive a condition of equality of ideas between partners are more likely to show a positive racial attitude change. The pupils whose teacher's behavior is judged as definitely supportive of friendly interracial contact have a more positive racial attitude change. Several other aspects of the Activity Group Program--attitude toward the interracial activity, perceptions of the skill of the teacher and the discussion leader, and the prior attitudes of the pupil toward his class and teacher--are found to be unrelated to racial attitude change.

CHAPTER 10

CHAPTER **10** SUMMARY AND
CONCLUSIONS

This chapter discusses the findings of the study
in three parts. The first part concerns the extent
to which racial attitudes depend on differences in
race, sex, age, and reading ability. The second part
contains an analysis of the effect of the Activity
Group Program in terms of the treatment group comparisons formulated in the hypotheses. The third
part contains an evaluation of the influence of various aspects of the Activity Group Program on attitude change.

FACTORS AFFECTING RACIAL ATTITUDES

Race

Previous research has indicated differences in
the racial attitudes of Negro and white people. The
white person has tended to view the Negro unfavorably
and to attribute undesirable characteristics to him.
The white person has shown reluctance to enter into
close relationships with Negro people. The Negro
person, on the other hand, has tended to describe
white people with desirable qualities and to devalue
his own race. The Negro person has shown more willingness to associate intimately with the white person

In the present investigation, the results of the
initial testing are similar to previous findings.
Negro pupils have significantly more favorable attitudes toward and greater willingness to associate
with white people than the white pupils have toward
Negro people. Both Negro and white pupils have racial attitudes favoring white people and devaluing
Negro people. The congruency of racial attitudes
between Negro and white pupils is consistent with
the evidence that members of less-favored groups
come to share the widely accepted standards concerning racial groups. Other studies have shown Negro

acceptance of white standards. For instance, the
Clarks found that a majority of Negro children preferred a white doll and rejected a colored doll.[1]
Also, Bayton's investigation showed that Negro college students and white Princeton University students
gave similar stereotypes concerning Negro people.[2]

In the present study Negro and white children
attend segregated schools. Therefore, apparently,
racial attitudes have been acquired more by contact
with prevalent attitudes in the culture than by di-
rect experience with members of the other race.
Negro and white pupils have learned to accept the
majority view that the white group is more desirable
than the Negro group.

Sex

Previous research has found that boys and girls
have similar racial attitudes. In the present investigation there are no significant differences in the
racial attitudes of boys and girls of the same race.
However, in some cases the differences in racial
attitude between Negro and white pupils are due
largely to differences among members of the same sex.
For example, fourth-grade Negro girls have significantly more favorable attitudes toward white people
than white girls have toward Negro people. In the
present study racial attitudes appear to reflect
race differences rather than sex differences.

Age

Interest has been shown in the chronological
development of racial attitudes. Several studies
have found changes in racial attitudes with increased
age. For example, Radke et al. found that sixth-
grade Negro children became more hostile toward the
white group and had more positive feelings toward
their own race than younger children.[3] In the present study, although it is considered desirable to
treat the results of the fourth- and fifth-grades
separately, similarities in the two grades are
noted. The fourth- and fifth-grade pupils show the
same direction in racial attitudes. Negro fourth-
and fifth-grade pupils have more favorable attitudes
toward white people than fourth- and fifth-grade
white pupils have toward Negro people. Pupils in
both grades and races favor the white group and
negate the Negro group. It appears that age

differences between fourth- and fifth-grade pupils
do not result in changes of racial attitude.

The present investigation studies the relationship between age and racial attitude within each
grade level. There are no significant correlations
between age and racial attitude for fourth-grade
Negro, fifth-grade white, or fifth-grade Negro pupils.
The only significant correlation is a positive one
among fourth-grade white pupils. This correlation
is barely significant at the .05 level. Apparently,
like age differences between grades, age within the
fourth and fifth gardes has little influence on racial attitudes.

Reading Ability

The present study explores the relationship
between reading achievement level and racial attitude.
There is a significant positive correlation between
reading ability and racial attitudes for fourth-grade
Negro pupils in the initial testing. Superior reading ability is related to a more favorable attitude
toward white people, a greater willingness to associate with them, and a corresponding devaluing of
Negroes. There are no significant correlations
between reading ability and initial racial attitudes
for the other pupil categories--fourth-grade white,
fifth-grade Negro, and fifth-grade white pupils.
Apparently, the better Negro readers in the fourth-
grade are more closely identified with the prevailing racial attitudes of the white group. They appear
to have adopted middle class attitudes toward achievement and race relations.

EFFECTS OF INTERRACIAL CONTACT

The second section of the discussion is an
analysis of the effect of the Activity Group Program
in terms of the hypothesized comparisons of attitude
change between treatment groups. The three hypotheses consist of the following comparisons of Negro
and white pupils' attitude change: (1) interracial
contact groups compared to no contact groups; (2)
interracial trip contact groups compared to interracial discussion contact groups; and (3) combined
interracial trip contact and discussion contact
groups compared to one or the other. The only hypothesis supported is the comparison of attitude
change of fifth-grade Negro pupils in the combined

interracial trip and discussion treatment (J-J group) with the attitude change of fifth-grade Negro pupils in either the interracial trip (J-S) or the interracial discussion (S-J) groups. On the Attitude Scale the combined treatment shows significantly greater positive attitude change than either of the other treatment groups. In the significant comparison between the fifth-grade Negro groups, the combined treatment group (J-J) shows a positive mean change Attitude Scale score, while the J-S and S-J have negative mean change scores. The contrasting attitude changes could be attributed to the differences in the types of interracial contact experienced by the respective treatment groups. Previous studies have indicated that the Negro child may experience feelings of uncertainty and hostility in contact with white children. In the present study trip observers report that pupils of both races frequently move away from their assigned other race partner back to their own classmates. There are indications of caution and guardedness between interracial partners. In the more abbreviated interracial contact of the fifth-grade Negro J-S and S-J groups, partner contact may have been so short-lived that Negro pupils do not have enough opportunity to change their initial negative reactions. In the fifth-grade Negro J-J group, however, the more extended interracial contact in both Trip and Discussion Activities helps the pupils overcome their apprehension and become more favorable toward their white partners. Data from the Trip Rating Sheets do, in fact, indicate that pupils in the fifth-grade Negro J-J group perceive their white partners more favorably than do the Negro pupils in the J-S and S-J groups.

The significant difference in the attitude changes of fifth-grade Negro pupils may have been due to two other factors in the study: namely, differences in reading and initial attitude scores. First, analysis of the reading scores of fifth-grade Negro pupils reveals significant differences between treatment groups. The mean reading score of pupils in the J-J group is significantly higher than the mean reading scores of the J-S and S-J groups. The positive correlation of reading scores and Attitude Scale change scores is significant at the .01 level for fifth-grade Negro pupils. Thus it could be argued that the significantly greater positive change of attitudes found in the fifth-grade Negro J-J group compared to the J-S and S-J groups is not due solely to the differences in experimental treatment.

Instead, the change could be partly explained by the
significant positive relationship between reading
ability and attitude change.

Second, although Scheffé's Multiple Comparisons
Test reveals no significant difference between the
pre-Attitude Scale scores of the fifth-grade Negro
treatment groups, it is observed that the pre-mean
score of the J-J group is lower than the mean scores
of the J-S and S-J groups. Thus the differences in
pre-score could be presented as an explanation of
the significant differences in change scores.

To control for the influence of reading the pre-
test scores, multiple analyses of covariance are
done, using reading and pre-scores as concomitant
variables. Results reveal that the previous significant differences (.01 level) between the change
scores of the fifth-grade Negro groups (J-J vs. J-S
and J-J vs. S-J) are not found using the adjusted
post-test scores. Therefore, when reading and pre-
attitude scores are controlled, no support is found
for any of the treatment comparisons formulated in
the hypotheses.

In general, the small number of pupils in each
treatment group and the large variances found in
attitude scores place restrictions on the possibilities of finding significant differences between
groups. Also, the unequal number of pupils in the
treatment groups require the use of Scheffé's
Multiple Comparisons Test to determine significance.
The extremely conservative nature of Scheffé's Test
limits the possibilities of significant differences.

INFLUENCE OF CONDITIONS OF INTERRACIAL CONTACT

The third chapter of the discussion analyzes
the influence of various aspects of the Activity
Group Program on attitude change. Cook's description of the interracial contact situation provides
the model for analyzing the Activity Group Program.

Acquaintance Potential

The influence of the first dimension, acquaintance potential, is seen in an examination of the
interracial partner relationship. Data from the
Trip Rating Sheet presents the pupils' perceptions
of the interracial partner contact. Item 2 refers

to the pupils' feelings about continued assignment
to the same partner. A positive response, wanting
the same partner for subsequent trips, signifies
satisfaction with contact. The positive response
further suggests that partners like each other,
enjoy the experience of contact, and develop a positive relationship. Conversely, a negative response,
the rejection of the same partner for subsequent
trips, signifies dissatisfaction with the contact.
The negative response further suggests that partners
do not like each other or the experience of the contact. Results from Item 2 show that among pupils in
interracial contact who change positively toward the
other race, a large majority (83 per cent) indicate
a desire to continue with the same partner. While
among pupils in interracial contact who change negatively toward the other race, less than half (48 per
cent) express a desire to continue with the same
partner. Thus the reaction of a Negro or white
pupil to contact with an assigned partner of the
other race seems to have considerable influence on
racial attitude change. Pupils who experience satisfying interracial contact are more likely to have a
positive change of attitude toward the other race.
The above finding demonstrates the significance of
Cook's dimension of acquaintance potential in inducing positive change of attitude.

Relative Status of the Participants

The role of Cook's second dimension, relative
status of the participants in interracial contact,
is also seen in the analysis of the interracial
partner relationship. Data from the Trip Rating
Sheets presents the pupils' perceptions of the interracial partner contact. Item 3 refers to the
pupils' evaluations of their own ideas compared to
those of their partners. A response indicating
equality between both ideas signifies a perception
of equal status between partners. In terms of the
equality of ideas, the relationship is seen as consisting of equal members. Conversely, a response of
inequality between both ideas signifies that the
pupil has perceived the partner relationship as made
up of unequal members. Results from Item 3 show
that among pupils in interracial contact who change
positively toward the other race, an overwhelming percentage (95) indicate a perception of equality between partners. Whereas, among pupils in interracial
contact who change negatively toward the other race
only slightly more than half (52 per cent) perceive

a condition of equality between partners. Thus the
Negro or white pupil's perception of the existence
of equality between himself and his partner of the
other race is another influence on racial attitude
change. Pupils who experience interracial contact
on an equal status level are more likely to change
positively toward the other race. The results demonstrate the importance of Cook's dimension concerning
the relative status of the participants in an interracial contact situation.

Social Norm Toward Interracial Contact

The study also presents evidence concerning
Cook's third dimension, the social norm toward interracial contact. Data from the observations of teacher
behavior during the Activity Group Program are judged
according to the degree of support provided for
friendly interracial contact. The behavior of only
one teacher (fifth-grade Negro J-J group) is judged
as definitely supportive of friendly interracial
contact. Results from the change scores of the
Attitude Scale reveal that the fifth-grade Negro J-J
group is the only group providing any support for
the hypotheses in the study. Attitude Scale change
scores indicate that Hypothesis 3 is supported at
the .01 level. The fifth-grade Negro J-J group shows
significantly greater positive change in racial attitudes than do either the fifth-grade Negro J-S or
S-J groups. Although the finding is limited to one
teacher and one group, it suggests the importance of
the teacher's behavior in establishing a norm that
facilitates friendly interracial contact.

Attitude Toward the Trip Experience

The study also provides data concerning the
relationship between reactions to the general activity in which the interracial activity occurred and
attitude change. Data from the Trip Rating Sheet
indicate that the preponderance of pupils, regardless
of whether their attitudes change negatively or positively toward the other race, have a positive
reaction to the trip experience. Only 4 per cent
of pupils who show a positive attitude change and
7 per cent who have a negative change express a dislike for the trip experiences. Thus the general
activity in which interracial contact occurs does
not influence the attitude toward members of the
other race. The specific reaction to the member of
the other race, rather than to the general activity,

is an influential factor in determining whether positive attitude change will be induced.

Attitude Toward Skill of Authority Figures

Results from the Activity Group Program provide
further evidence concerning the role of authority
persons in interracial contact situations. Data are
presented regarding the influence on pupils' attitude
change of the authority persons' skill in carrying
out the activities of the program. Items 1 and 2 of
the Teacher-Discussion Leader Rating Sheet indicate
that the skill of authority persons in the interracial
activities is unrelated to racial attitude change.
Negative change of attitude is as frequent as positive
change among pupils who perceive the teachers and
discussion leaders as highly skilled.

Attitude Toward Own Teacher and Classmates

The present study presents further clarification
of other aspects of the pupil interracial contact.
Data collected from the pupils clarifies the relationship between classroom attitudes existing before
interracial contact and racial attitude change as a
result of interracial contact. Analysis of responses
to items of My Teacher, Classroom Life, and How This
Class Thinks shows a lack of differentiation between
pupils whose racial attitudes change negatively and
those whose attitudes change positively. Thus the
feelings a Negro or white child has toward his class
and teacher are unrelated to racial attitude change
through interracial contact.

To briefly summarize the discussion, the present
investigation finds that the racial attitudes of
fourth- and fifth-grade Negro and white pupils are
consistent with previous findings. The Negro pupils
have more favorable attitudes toward white people
than white people have toward Negro people. Negro
and white pupils favor white people and devalue
Negro people. There are no sex differences in the
racial attitudes of pupils of the same race. Prior
to interracial contact, superior reading ability
among fourth-grade Negro pupils is related to a more
positive evaluation of white people. Using change
scores, the only support for the hypotheses is the
greater positive change of attitude in fifth-grade
Negro pupils who experience interracial trip and
discussion contact compared to those who experience
one or the other. There is a positive relationship

between reading ability and racial attitude change
among fifth-grade Negro pupils. No support for the
hypotheses is found when reading and pre-test attitude scores are controlled. Each of Cook's dimen-
sions--acquaintance potential, relative status of the
participants in interracial contact, and the social
norm toward interracial contact--is an influential
factor in racial attitude change. Other factors--
attitude toward the trip, perception of the skill of
teachers and discussion leaders, and previous attitudes toward class and teacher--are found to be unrelated to racial attitude change.

AREAS FOR FUTURE RESEARCH

The findings of the study provide evidence that
under certain conditions face-to-face contact between
Negro and white pupils exerts a positive influence
on racial attitudes. It would appear that greater
changes might occur with more intensive and extensive
interracial contact. Future investigations should
include more contact.

Since the subjects in the study are fourth- and
fifth-grade pupils in New York City, the question of
whether the findings apply to other age groups and
in other localities would require further investigation.

The families and neighborhood characteristics
in each of the school areas suggest the possibility
of socioeconomic differences between the two racial
groups in the study. The influence of socioeconomic
differences on the pupils' perceptions of each other
in the Activity Group Program could be an area that
other studies might explore. Depth interviews with
subjects could be designed to elicit information
concerning the significance of any socioeconomic differences. Further research might also include interracial programs with pupils of similar socioeconomic
backgrounds.

In the present study only two of the 16 teachers
are Negro. It is unknown how much the imbalance of
Negro and white teachers affected the results of the
present research. The influence of the race of the
teacher should be studied in future research.

There are differences among the three instruments used in the present study to measure racial

attitudes. Two of the instruments, the Attitude
Scale and the Social Distance Scale, openly refer to
specific racial groups. It is clear that the tests
are eliciting attitudes toward members of another
race. The third instrument, the Projective Picture
Test, requires no reading and involves the selection
of a photograph of a Negro or white person in response
to a descriptive statement. The directions and the
test do not use the words "Negro" or "white." It is
not clear that racial attitudes are being elicited.

The instruments may have measured different
aspects of racial attitudes. The Social Distance
Scale requires the respondent to indicate how much
intimacy he would accept with members of the other
race. The Attitude Scale consists of items similar
to those of the Social Distance Scale and others
eliciting general opinions about members of the other
race. The Projective Picture Test is projective in
that the respondent attributes behavioral descriptions to photographs of Negro and white children.

In future research other instruments might be
devised to measure racial attitudes. They could be
disguised as to purpose and depend as little as possible on reading ability. In future short-term investigations similar to the present study, observational techniques might be used to compare pupils'
behavior in early interracial contacts with behavior
in later interracial contacts.

SUMMARY OF EXPERIMENT

Background

Interest in racial relations in the schools and
the influence of the interracial contact situation
on racial attitudes led the investigator to develop
this exploratory field study.

Problem

The main problem of the study was to determine
the effectiveness of a school Activity Group Program
in inducing positive change in the racial attitudes
of Negro and white children from selected elementary
schools in New York City. In the Activity Group
Program two types of interracial contact--a field
trip and a discussion experience--were experimentally

manipulated so that the cumulative and separate effects of the two experiences could be evaluated.

Focus of Study

The study focused on the influence of six conditions of the interracial contact: (1) satisfaction
with interracial contact; (2) the relative status of
the participants; (3) the social norm toward contact
of one group with another; (4) the attitude toward
the general activity of interracial contact; (5) the
perception of the skill of teachers and discussion
leaders; and (6) the previous attitudes toward own
class and teacher.

Experiemental Procedure

Fourth- and fifth-grade Negro and white pupils
from two racially segregated schools in New York City
participated in the Activity Group Program. The
subjects were in sixteen classes, four fourth-grade
classes and four fifth-grade classes from each of
the schools. By controlling the assignment of partners of the same grade level and sex, four experimental treatments of different degrees of interracial
contact were organized. Certain classes experienced
interracial contact during both the Trip and Discussion Activities, other experienced interracial contact
only for Trip or Discussion Activity, and the remainder were not exposed to interracial contact at all.
Two fourth-grade classes, one from each school, and
two fifth-grade classes, one from each school, were
assigned to one of the four experimental treatments
of different interracial contact.

Hypotheses

Three hypotheses were formulated: (1) pupils
in treatment groups experiencing interracial contact
would show significantly greater positive changes in
racial attitude than would pupils experiencing no
interracial contact; (2) pupils in treatment groups
experiencing trip contact would show significantly
greater positive changes in racial attitude than
would pupils experiencing interracial discussion
contact; and (3) pupils in treatment groups experiencing both interracial trip contact and discussion
contact would show significantly greater positive
changes in racial attitude than would pupils experiencing either interracial trip or interracial discussion contact.

Procedures in Collecting Data

Three measures of racial attitudes were used--
the Attitude Scale, the Social Distance Scale, and
the Projective Picture Test. Supplementary tests--
My Teacher, Classroom Life, and How This Class
Thinks--were used to measure the pupils' perceptions
of life in their classrooms. Rating Sheets were
devised to gather data regarding the pupils' perceptions of their partners and other aspects of the
Activity Group Program. Additional data were gathered
from observations of teacher and pupil behavior.

Findings

None of the hypotheses were supported in the
fourth grade for Negro or white pupils. In the fifth
grade, Hypothesis 3 was supported for fifth-grade
Negro pupils on the Attitude Scale. Fifth-grade
Negro pupils who experienced interracial trip and
discussion contact showed significantly greater positive change of racial attitude than did fifth-grade
Negro pupils who experienced either interracial trip
or interracial discussion contact. When the analysis
of the data was controlled for differences in reading
ability and initial attitudes, none of the hypotheses
were supported.

The following factors in interracial contact
were found to have an influence on racial attitude
change: (1) satisfaction with interracial contact;
(2) the relative status of the participants; and
(3) the social norm toward contact. Other factors--
attitude toward the trip, perception of the skill of
teachers and discussion leaders, and previous attitudes toward own class and teacher--were found to be
unrelated to racial attitude change.

NOTES

1. Kenneth B. Clark and Mamie P. Clark,
"Racial Identification and Preference in Negro
Children", in Eleanor E. Maccoby, Theodore M.
Newcomb, and Eugene L. Hartley eds., Readings in
Social Psychology (New York: Henry Holt and Co.,
1958), p. 602-11.

2.   James A. Bayton, "The Racial Stereotypes of Negro College Students," Journal of Abnormal and Social Psychology, XXXVI (1941), 99-102.

3.   Marian Radke, Jean Sutherland, and Pearl Rosenberg, "Racial Attitudes of Children," Sociometry, XIII (1950), 154-71.

CHAPTER **11** IMPLICATIONS FOR
INTERRACIAL CONTACT
THEORY AND EDUCATIONAL
PRACTICE

The interracial field experiment with children
from two segregated schools is of importance in
several respects. First, it contributes to the findings on interracial contact theory. Specifically,
the study tests the influence of certain conditions
of interracial contact on positive racial attitude
change. Second, the study describes the process of
conducting an interracial program in the school system. The study highlights many of the problems involved in effectively carrying out an interracial
program. Third, observer reports during actual interracial contact offer a dramatic firsthand description of what happens when Negro and white children
come together.

The findings concerning the influence of the
personal relationship between Negro and white children on attitude change offer implications for programs of interracial contact. Simply bringing Negro
and white children together in the same situation
is not enough to induce positive racial attitude
change. In general, children left to their own de-
vices will gravitate toward classmates of their own
race. Many integrated situations make no provision
for the development of personal relationships between
Negro and white children. As Deutsch has pointed
out, "There are too many children who sit in a segregated island in a so-called integrated classroom,
with there being no real attempt to help the children
establish some intergroup, interpersonal knowledge
and relationship."[1]

Observations during the activity group program
indicate that children may be fearful, hostile, or
resistant in an interracial contact situation. It
has been suggested that children's fears and attempts
to withdraw from a new situation are due to lack of

knowledge and misconceptions about elements of the
situation.[2] This is particularly true of the interracial contact situation. Negro and white children
from segregated schools lack experience in interracial
contact. Their knowledge of each other may be based
on narrow stereotypes.[3] Therefore, it is important
that interracial contact situations provide experiences that reduce apprehension, increase interpersonal knowledge, and result in individual satisfaction. This can be done prior to actual contact
whether the interracial contact is to take place in
an activity group program or in a newly integrated
school. Children who are about to enter an interracial contact situation should be prepared in various ways. Negro and white children can exchange
class and individual photographs to become acquainted
and learn about each other. Individual photographs
showing children in different activities can help
children to share experiences and identify mutual
interests. Negro and white children can exchange
information concerning class and individual activities. Taped music experiences and favorite class
songs can be shared. Special art projects can be
exchanged. Written descriptions or tapes of class
discussions can provide information about the pupils.
For example, one shared discussion may concern
problems with younger or older siblings.

   Negro and white pupils can exchange letters
describing their preferences in sports, music,
dancing, movies, television programs, books, clothes,
and games. Pupil weekly time budgets including hours
spent watching television, playing games, doing home-
work, helping in the home, sleeping, etc., can be
shared.

   During actual interracial contact, plans must
be made for the Negro and white children to build
intergroup and interpersonal knowledge and relationships. In the interracial situation, structures
must be established to build a bridge between Negro
and white children. It must be clear that the Negro
and white pupils constitute one group, rather than
two separate groups. Communication channels must
be set up between Negro and white children. The
field study established partner assignments during
interracial contact as one method to achieve this
purpose. The partners walked together, ate together,
worked together, and talked informally together.
Other methods to develop personal relationships

between Negro and white children can be interracial
play groups, committees, teams, and buddy systems.

In the school interracial contact situation,
activities must be organized to help Negro and white
children get to know each other and develop satisfying personal relationships. Deutsch suggests the
use of a simple autobiographical method in a newly
integrated classroom, where each child tells something about himself and his interests and aspira-
tions.[4] In general, the atmosphere of the classroom
should emphasize cooperation. Competition tends to
divide. Structures should be provided where children
can informally work and play together. Formality
tends to inhibit the development of intimacy. The
classroom should be conducted so that Negro and white
children can come to view each other as equal status
members of the interracial contact situation. Efforts
should be made to minimize Negro and white differences
that tend to reinforce negative stereotypes. For
example, if there are marked academic differences between Negro and white children, varied opportunities
to interact in informal, nonacademic activities, such
as music, art, dramatizations, and athletics, must
be provided. If the Negro and white children repre-
sent different socioeconomic classes, as they do in
the field experiment, educational experiences should
be provided that can help children to realize that
there are Negroes and whites at all points on the
economic scale. For example, Negro and white children can participate together in a drive to help white
poverty-stricken Appalachian families. Or the Negro
and white children can organize a program to invite
and meet Negro and white lawyers, artists, and businessmen.

The present study has indicated the importance
of the attitudes and the behavior of school administrators and teachers in carrying out an effective
interracial contact program. Integration requires
a change in shcool procedures. A newly integrated
school should have an environment receptive to experiment and change. It should have the flexibility to
incorporate new procedures. There should be a commitment to the improvement of relations between the
races. Principals and other supervisory personnel
play a crucial role in providing the proper school
atmosphere. Administrators must be open to change,
ready to try new approaches, and personally committed
to improving the relations between the races.

Administrators who fear that such a program would
cause staff resentment, who are indifferent to the
goal of improved interracial relations, who fear opposition from parents, and who want to conform to the
status quo are inimical to a successful integration
program.

The importance of the teacher cannot be over-
emphasized. The teacher sets the tone of social
relationships between Negro and white children. She
determines what is to be rewarded and what punished.
She influences what the general reactions will be of
one racial group toward the other. She is the living model of right behavior.

Evidence from the field experiment indicates
that many teachers will express resistance or indif-
ference to an interracial program. Therefore, it is
of the utmost importance for the success of planned
school interracial situations that procedures be
established to train teachers and administrators to
new attitudes and behaviors. On a pre-service level,
schools of education must require their graduates to
have adequate training in the history of minorities,
cultural anthropology, and the behavioral sciences.
Teacher education programs must reflect a pattern of
preparation which includes laboratory and course
experiences designed to enable teachers to work effectively and sensitively with children from cul-
turally different groups. On the in-service level,
administrators and teachers must be helped to gain
greater awareness and understanding of the needs
and problems of children of varying racial, ethnic,
and cultural backgrounds. They must be helped to
examine their own racial attitudes, their misconceptions about minority group children, and their
fears in relation to the interracial situation. The
basic unit of such a training program would involve
weekly meetings in small discussion groups conducted
by a human relations specialist. Participants would
begin to discuss their own feelings, reactions, and
behavior in the area of race relations. Specific
teacher responses and practices would be analyzed
and evaluated in regard to effects on children of
both races. For example, ways in which teachers
handle questions of race and intergroup relations
in the classroom and their effects on children would
be examined. The effects on Negro and white children
of an objective, frank, professional approach as compared to embarrassment and avoidance would be explored.

These small group discussions would focus on the teachers' feelings and behavior in the inter-racial situation. Teachers' reactions to specific problems between Negro and white children would be discussed. Teachers would take the part of a Negro or white child in role-playing to gain insight into children's feelings. New teacher behavior would be tried out to develop skill in various situations. A number of situations that developed in the field experiment would be the type of interracial problem that would be discussed and analyzed for appropriate teacher behavior. For example, there were occasions in which Negro and white pupils refused to join and work with their partners. There were instances of arguments and fights between children of both races. In one interracial situation a Negro boy broke into an angry outburst toward another Negro boy using the insult, "white creep". On another occasion when the Negro and white children met, Negro pupils teased a white boy calling him, "white fat," and Negro girls teased a white girl saying, "She's white."

The field experiment provided evidence of par-ent fear and resistance to the interracial contact program. Parent influence on pupil behavior was seen when children refused to answer trip question-aires and attitude tests saying, "My mother told me not to take any more tests." There was a suggestion from a teacher in the white school that a pupil in her class was kept home from one of the trips be-cause of parent concern. As has been pointed out, an effective school interracial program must have community and parent support.[5] Organizations and individuals in the community--clergy, politicians, P.T.A., businessmen, newspaper editors, labor leaders, and parents--should be involved. Parent associations should organize parent committees to help plan and implement interracial programs. Mixed parent-teacher groups should meet to discuss problems and ideas to make the program more effective. Negro and white parents should meet together to further the goals of the interracial program. Community representa-tives of civic, religious, and business organizations should meet with school personnel to coordinate their activities to help create a readiness for, an acceptance of, and a commitment to interracial pro-grams.

NOTES

1.   Martin Deutsch, "Dimensions of the School's Role in the Problems of Integration," in Gordon J. Klopf and Israel A. Laster, eds., Integrating the Urban School: Proceedings of the Conference on Integration in the New York City Public Schools. (New York: Teachers College, Columbia University, 1963), P. 35.

2.   George G. Thompson, Child Psychology. (Boston: Houghton Mifflin, 1962).

3.   Marian Radke and Jean Sutherland, "Children's Concepts About Minority and Majority American Groups," Journal of Educational Psychology, XL (1949), 449-68.

4.   Martin Deutsch, "Dimensions of the School's Role in the Problems of Integration," op. cit., pp. 29-44.

5.   Daniel C. Thompson, "Our Wasted Potential," in Gordon J. Klopf and Israel A. Laster, eds., Integrating the Urban School: Proceedings of the Conference on Integration in the New York City Public Schools. (New York: Teachers College, Columbia University, 1963), pp. 1-11; and Bonita Valien, "Community in Chaos, Cairo, Illinois," in Robin M. Williams and Margaret W. Ryan, eds., Schools in Transition: Community Experience in Desegregation. (Chapel Hill: The University of North Carolina Press, 1954), pp. 80-110.

APPENDIXES

APPENDIX A

MEANS, STANDARD DEVIATIONS, TESTS OF SIGNIFICANCE,
AND GRADE EQUIVALENTS FOR READING SCORES
OF NEGRO AND WHITE SUBJECTS

TABLE 1

Means and Standard Deviations of Reading Raw Scores* of
Fourth-Grade Negro and White Pupils by Experimental
Treatment Groups

Experimental Treatment	School A--Negro Pupils (N = 66)		School B--White Pupils (N = 62)	
	Word Knowledge	Reading	Word Knowledge	Reading
J-J				
Mean	41.95	34.37	39.76	35.57
Standard Deviation	5.86	5.93	5.42	5.75
Number	19	19	21	21
J-S				
Mean	25.50	21.25	31.54	24.69
Standard Deviation	7.67	6.52	7.09	6.97
Number	16	16	13	13
S-J				
Mean	16.00	14.35	25.62	20.69
Standard Deviation	4.80	2.67	5.38	6.99
Number	17	17	16	16
S-S				
Mean	12.50	12.14	19.75	12.17
Standard Deviation	5.02	4.69	7.53	5.64
Number	14	14	12	12
Totals				
Mean	25.03	21.32	30.52	24.92
Standard Deviation	13.14	10.31	9.78	10.67

*Metropolitan Achievement Test, Elementary Reading Test, Form B.

TABLE 2

Scheffé's Multiple Comparisons Test of Word Knowledge and Reading
for Fourth-Grade Negro and White Pupils

Group Comparisons	Word Knowledge				Reading			
	Negro Difference in Means	Significance Level	White Difference in Means	Significance Level	Negro Difference in Means	Significance Level	White Difference in Means	Significance Level
J-J vs. J-S	16.45	.01	8.22	.05	13.12	.01	10.88	.01
J-J vs. S-J	25.95	.01	14.14	.01	20.02	.01	14.88	.01
J-J vs. S-S	29.45	.01	20.01	.01	22.23	.01	23.40	.01
J-S vs. S-J	9.50	.01	5.92	ns	6.90	ns	4.00	ns
J-S vs. S-S	13.00	.01	11.79	.01	9.11	.05	12.52	.01
S-J vs. S-S	4.50	ns	5.87	ns	2.21	ns	8.52	.05
Msw	37.05				33.30			

Group Comparisons	Word Knowledge		Reading	
	Differences between Negro and White Means	Significance Level	Differences between Negro and White Means	Significance Level
J-J vs. J-J	2.19	ns	1.20	ns
J-S vs. J-S	6.04	ns	3.44	ns
S-J vs. S-J	9.62	.01	6.34	ns
S-S vs. S-S	7.25	ns	.03	ns
Msw	37.05		33.30	

TABLE 3

Means of Reading Scores* in Grade Equivalents of Fourth-Grade Negro and White Pupils by Experimental Treatment Groups

| Experimental Treatment | School A--Negro Pupils (N = 66) | | School B--White Pupils (N = 62) | |
	Word Knowledge	Reading	Word Knowledge	Reading
J-J				
Mean	6.4	5.2	5.9	5.4
Range	3.6-9.6	3.5-11.4	3.7-7.7	3.4-9.0
Number	19	19	21	21
J-S				
Mean	3.8	3.5	4.4	4.0
Range	2.9-5.7	2.8-5.9	3.2-6.4	3.0-5.5
Number	16	16	13	13
S-J				
Mean	3.0	3.0	3.8	3.5
Range	2.2-3.6	2.6-3.5	2.9-4.7	2.7-5.3
Number	17	17	16	16
S-S				
Mean	2.7	2.8	3.2	2.8
Range	1.8-3.3	1.8-3.5	2.1-4.9	1.9-3.6
Number	14	14	12	12
Totals				
Mean	3.7	3.5	4.3	4.0
Range	1.8-9.6	1.8-11.4	2.1-7.7	1.9-9.0

*Metropolitan Achievement Test, Elementary Reading Test, Form B.

TABLE 4

Means and Standard Deviations of Reading Raw Scores* of
Fifth-Grade Negro and White Pupils by Experimental
Treatment Groups

Experimental Treatment		School A--Negro Pupils (N = 55)		School B--White Pupils (N = 60)	
		Word Knowledge	Reading	Word Knowledge	Reading
J-J	Mean	24.50	18.83	32.90	21.52
	Standard Deviation	7.16	5.58	8.18	4.47
	Number	18	18	21	21
J-S	Mean	10.00	11.75	33.21	20.57
	Standard Deviation	4.91	3.61	5.63	3.69
	Number	16	16	14	14
S-J	Mean	9.44	11.56	23.23	15.08
	Standard Deviation	5.75	3.84	7.88	4.42
	Number	9	9	13	13
S-S	Mean	7.42	10.67	17.50	12.08
	Standard Deviation	3.80	4.79	5.73	2.81
	Number	12	12	12	12
Totals	Mean	14.09	13.80	27.80	18.02
	Standard Deviation	9.23	5.74	9.53	5.50

*Metropolitan Achievement Test, Intermediate Reading Test, Form Bm.

148

TABLE 5

Scheffé's Multiple Comparisons Test of Word Knowledge and Reading
for Fifth-Grade Negro and White Pupils

Group Comparisons	Word Knowledge				Reading			
	Negro Difference in Means	Significance Level	White Difference in Means	Significance Level	Negro Difference in Means	Significance Level	White Difference in Means	Significance Level
J-J vs. J-S	14.50	.01	.30	ns	7.08	.01	.95	ns
J-J vs. S-J	15.06	.01	9.67	.05	7.27	.05	6.44	.05
J-J vs. S-S	17.08	.01	15.40	.01	8.16	.01	9.44	.01
J-S vs. S-J	.56	ns	9.98	.05	.19	ns	5.49	ns
J-S vs. S-S	2.58	ns	15.71	.01	1.08	ns	8.49	.01
S-J vs. S-S	2.02	ns	5.73	ns	.89	ns	3.00	ns
Msw	42.18				18.63			

Group Comparisons	Word Knowledge		Reading	
	Differences between Negro and White Means	Significance Level	Differences between Negro and White Means	Significance Level
J-J vs. J-J	8.40	.05	2.69	ns
J-S vs. J-S	23.21	.01	8.82	.01
S-J vs. S-J	13.79	.01	3.52	ns
S-S vs. S-S	10.08	ns	1.41	ns
Msw	42.18		18.63	

149

TABLE 6

Means of Reading Scores* in Grade Equivalents of Fifth-Grade Negro and White Pupils by Experimental Treatment Groups

Experimental Treatment	School A--Negro Pupils (N = 55)		School B--White Pupils (N = 60)	
	Word Knowledge	Reading	Word Knowledge	Reading
J-J				
Mean	5.1	5.3	6.2	5.8
Range	3.7-8.2	3.5-8.4	4.5-8.5	4.1-9.0
Number	18	18	21	21
J-S				
Mean	3.1	3.9	6.2	5.6
Range	3.0-5.0	3.0-5.5	5.0-8.2	4.2-7.0
Number	16	16	14	14
S-J				
Mean	3.0	3.8	4.9	4.4
Range	3.0-4.5	3.0-5.1	3.1-6.5	3.0-5.9
Number	9	9	13	13
S-S				
Mean	3.0	3.6	4.3	3.9
Range	3.0-3.4	3.0-4.6	3.1-5.5	3.0-4.9
Number	12	12	12	12
Totals				
Mean	3.7	4.2	5.5	5.1
Range	3.0-8.2	3.0-8.4	3.1-8.5	3.0-9.0

*Metropolitan Achievement Test, Intermediate Reading Test, Form Bm.

APPENDIX B

MEANS, STANDARD DEVIATIONS, AND TESTS OF
SIGNIFICANCE FOR AGES OF NEGRO AND
WHITE SUBJECTS

TABLE 7

Means and Standard Deviations of Ages in Months
of Fourth-Grade Negro and White Pupils by
Experimental Treatment Groups

Experimental Treatment		School A Negro Pupils (N = 66)	School B White Pupils (N = 62)
J-J	Mean	113.37	111.29
	Standard Deviation	7.41	4.76
	Number	19	21
J-S	Mean	111.00	111.54
	Standard Deviation	3.72	4.91
	Number	16	13
S-J	Mean	114.59	111.00
	Standard Deviation	6.46	4.37
	Number	17	16
S-S	Mean	115.14	117.25
	Standard Deviation	6.41	8.87
	Number	14	12
Totals	Mean	113.48	112.42
	Standard Deviation	6.27	6.06

TABLE 8

Scheffé's Multiple Comparisons Test of Age for
Fourth-Grade Negro and White Pupils

| | Age | | | |
| | Negro | | White | |
Group Comparisons	Difference in Means	Significance Level	Difference in Means	Significance Level
J-J vs. J-S	2.37	ns	.25	ns
J-J vs. S-J	1.22	ns	.29	ns
J-J vs. S-S	1.77	ns	5.96	ns
J-S vs. S-J	3.59	ns	.54	ns
J-S vs. S-S	4.14	ns	5.71	ns
S-J vs. S-S	.55	ns	6.25	ns
Msw	35.77			

| | Age | |
Group Comparisons	Differences between Negro and White Means	Significance Level
J-J vs. J-J	2.08	ns
J-S vs. J-S	.54	ns
S-J vs. S-J	3.59	ns
S-S vs. S-S	2.11	ns
Msw	35.77	

TABLE 9

Means and Standard Deviations of Ages in Months
of Fifth-Grade Negro and White Pupils by
Experimental Treatment Groups

Experimental Treatment		School A Negro Pupils (N = 55)	School B White Pupils (N = 60)
J-J	Mean	123.83	122.57
	Standard Deviation	2.68	3.92
	Number	18	21
J-S	Mean	123.44	122.86
	Standard Deviation	3.39	5.20
	Number	16	14
S-J	Mean	129.11	122.92
	Standard Deviation	14.38	3.77
	Number	9	13
S-S	Mean	131.75	131.00
	Standard Deviation	6.69	6.92
	Number	12	12
Totals	Mean	126.31	124.40
	Standard Deviation	7.59	5.84

TABLE 10

Scheffé's Multiple Comparisons Test of Age for
Fifth-Grade Negro and White Pupils

| | Age | | | |
| | Negro | | White | |
Group Comparisons	Difference in Means	Significance Level	Difference in Means	Significance Level
J-J vs. J-S	.39	ns	.29	ns
J-J vs. S-J	5.28	ns	.35	ns
J-J vs. S-S	7.92	ns	8.43	.05
J-S vs. S-J	5.67	ns	.06	ns
J-S vs. S-S	8.31	ns	8.14	ns
S-J vs. S-S	2.64	ns	8.08	ns
Msw	35.49			

| | Age | |
Group Comparisions	Differences between Negro and White Means	Significance Level
J-J vs. J-J	1.26	ns
J-S vs. J-S	.58	ns
S-J vs. S-J	6.19	ns
S-S vs. S-S	.75	ns
Msw	35.49	

APPENDIX C

THE ATTITUDE SCALE, THE SOCIAL DISTANCE SCALE,
THE PROJECTIVE PICTURE TEST, SUPPLEMENTARY
TESTS, AND RATING SHEETS

ATTITUDE SCALE

Below are some sentences about Negro/white people.* In the column to the right of each sentence, check whether you agree or disagree with the sentence. Check the box marked <u>agree</u> if you agree with the sentence; check the box marked <u>disagree</u> if you do not agree with the sentence.

CHECK ONE BOX

1. They work hard.	agree	disagree
2. They make good teachers.	agree	disagree
3. I would like to live next door to them.	agree	disagree
4. I do not like them.	agree	disagree
5. It is easy to be friends with them.	agree	disagree
6. I would like to have them come to eat at my house.	agree	disagree
7. They are good neighbors.	agree	disagree
8. They often hurt other people's feelings.	agree	disagree
9. I would like to be in a club or in a team with them.	agree	disagree
10. They are always honest.	agree	disagree
11. They have done a lot to help our country.	agree	disagree
12. I would not want to ask any of them to a party.	agree	disagree
13. I would like to go on a picnic with them.	agree	disagree
14. They are pretty dumb.	agree	disagree
15. They get excited over little things.	agree	disagree
16. I would like to have one for my teacher next year.	agree	disagree
17. It is a waste of time and money to send them to college.	agree	disagree
18. I would like to see one of them get elected President of the United States.	agree	disagree

*One racial group was used depending on the race of the respondents.

Scoring

Responses were given a credit of +1 or 0. Scores were obtained by giving one point for each favorable statement with which a subject agreed and one point for each unfavorable statement with which a subject disagreed. The score was determined by adding up the points. The range of scores was 0 to +18. The score for each racial group reflected the attitude of the children toward the other race. The lower the score, the greater the degree of negative attitude toward the other race. The test differed only in the race specified in the directions.

Test Data

The authors developed the instrument through repeated use with pupils in grades three through six whose reading levels ranged from good to poor. A final scale was formed which covered a range of opinion from favorable to unfavorable (as judged by the pupils themselves), which discriminated between high and low scores, and which could be read and answered sensibly by all of the grade levels involved. The split-half reliability of the scale, even in the third-grade groups where reading problems would most seriously affect the results, was consistently at or above +.80. Gough et al. also found that the Attitude Scale significantly correlated with the results on a Personality Inventory administered during their investigation. There was differentiation between high and low scoring children on the Attitude Scale in their responses to the Personality Inventory items.

Using the Attitude Scale, Tabachnick's study showed a high negative correlation between prejudice and total satisfaction with self in more than 300 fifth-grade pupils.[1]

In the present study, the Attitude Scale was given twice, at an interval of two weeks, to fourth- and fifth-grade Negro and white pupils. The Negro pupils all came from one school with a heavy predominance of Negro pupils. The white pupils all came from one school with a heavy predominance of white pupils. There was a reliability coefficient of +.83 with 46 fourth- and fifth-grade white pupils. With 27 fourth- and fifth-grade Negro pupils there was a test-retest reliability coefficient of +.81.

SOCIAL DISTANCE SCALE

Below are the names of some groups of people--
the Chinese people, the Negro people, the white people, and the Japanese people. For each group of
people there are nine sentences to answer. When you
answer the sentences about each of these groups of
people, think of the people as a whole, not the best
or the worst ones you have known.

If you would do what the sentence says about a
group of people, place a check (√) in the column to
the right of the sentence. If you would not do what
the sentence says, don't put anything in the column.

I. The Chinese   Column

    1. I would let them visit our country. _____

    2. I would let them live in our
        country.   _____

    3. I would let them go to my school. _____

    4. I would let them live in my neigh-
        borhood.   _____

    5. I would let them live next door to
        me.   _____

    6. I would let them play at my house. _____

    7. I would let them come to a party
        at my house.   _____

    8. I would let them be my best
        friends.   _____

    9. I would be willing to marry one
        of them when I grow up.   _____

II. The Negroes   Column

    1. I would let them visit our country. _____

    2. I would let them live in our
        country.   _____

    3. I would let them go to my school. _____

Column

4. I would let them live in my neighborhood.   _____

5. I would let them live next door
   to me.   _____

6. I would let them play at my house.   _____

7. I would let them come to a party
   at my house.   _____

8. I would let them by my best
   friends.   _____

9. I would be willing to marry one of
   them when I grow up.   _____

III. The Whites   Column

1. I would let them visit our country. _____

2. I would let them live in our
   country.   _____

3. I would let them go to my school.   _____

4. I would let them live in my neighborhood.   _____

5. I would let them live next door to
   me.   _____

6. I would let them play at my house.   _____

7. I would let them come to a party at
   my house.   _____

8. I would let them be my best
   friends.   _____

9. I would be willing to marry one
   of them when I grow up.   _____

IV. The Japanese   Column

1. I would let them visit our country. _____

2. I would let them live in our
   country.   _____

3. I would let them go to my school.   _____

4. I would let them live in my neighborhood.   _____

5. I would let them live next door to
   me.   _____

6. I would let them play at my house.   _____

7. I would let the come to a party at
   my house.   _____

8. I would let them be my best
   friends.   _____

9. I would be willing to marry one of
   them when I grow up.   _____

Scoring

As Goode and Hatt state regarding the scoring
of the Social Distance Scale, ". . . the most practical method is to assign arbitrarily the values. . .
just as they are given for the statements. The sum
of the values thus obtained would equal the score
for the individual."[2] The scoring of the Social
Distance Scale was achieved by assigning the values
of 1 to 9 just as they are given for the statements.
For those statements with which the subject agreed,
he was given credit according to the value assigned
to those statements. The subject received 0 credit
for those statements with which he disagreed. The
sum of the values thus obtained was taken as the
score for the individual. The range of scores was
from 0 to +45. To disguise the purpose of the test,
the subjects were asked to respond to four groups,
namely, Chinese, Negro, white, and Japanese. Only
the score toward the white group was used for Negro
respondents and only the score toward the Negro
group was used for white respondents.

Test Data

The Social Distance Scale has been used exten-
sively in research. Campbell states:

> The Bogardus Social Distance Scale is
> probably the most used single test of
> social attitudes, with a popularity
> that shows no sign of waning. . .Among
> social attitude tests, the Social Dis-
> tance Scale is so good, and so natu-
> rally suited to its purpose, that if
> Bogardus had not invented it, someone
> else would have. Such a situation is
> rare indeed in the social sciences.[3]

Following Goode and Hatt's dictum that "the
test-retest approach is the most effective measure
of reliability of such a scale," the Social Distance
Scale was given twice to the same group of pupils
that was used to test the reliability of the Attitude Scale.[4] With 49 fourth- and fifth-grade white
pupils, a reliability coefficient of +.90 was found.
With 27 fourth- and fifth-grade Negro pupils, there
was a reliability coefficient of +.91.

PROJECTIVE PICTURE TEST

We are going to look at some pictures today.
It is going to be a game to see if you can tell what
people are like just by looking at their pictures.
It is not a test, but you are to try hard to do your
best.

We are going to look at pictures of boys and
girls whom you have not seen before. I'm going to
tell you about some of these children. Try to guess
which boy or girl I'm telling you about. When you
think you know which it is, put the answer on this
paper.

One of these children:

1. is the smartest in the school.

2. never bothers to do anything and is a very lazy
    child.

3. is very nice and kind.

4. is always shouting and yelling around the school
    yard.

5. is the bravest of anyone in school and helped
    put out a fire one day.

6. started a fight in the school yard.

7. is always neat and clean.

8. is not very smart and cannot answer any questions
    on tests.

9. has very nice manners.

10. pushes and crowds ahead of all the other child-
    ren in line into the movie house to try to get
    the best seat.

11. never fights if it can be helped, but usually
    wins if there is a fight.

12. stole an apple from the grocery yesterday.

13. is always fair and waits turn with the other
    children.

14. tore a book one day, but told the teacher some-
    body else tore it.

15. never swears or uses bad words.

16. always comes to school dirty.

17. always tries to do his or her best.

18. is very mean.

19. does not tell lies.

20. seems to be afraid of everything, even a shadow.

21. never shouts and screams when not supposed to.

22. has no manners at all; doesn't know how to
    behave.

23. found a purse on the bus with five dollars in
    it and gave it back to the person who lost it.

24. is always swearing and using bad words.

Scoring

The scoring was gained by taking the 24 responses for each subject and dividing them into four separate totals as follows: (a) the total number of positive statements given, white photographs; (b) the total number of negative statements given white photographs; (c) the total number of positive statements given Negro photographs; and (d) the total number of negative statements given Negro photographs.

The range on each of these separate totals (a, b, c, d) was from 0 to 12.   The number of Negro photographs selected could range from 0 to 24.   The number of white photographs selected could range from 0 to 24.

The scoring method used by Radke et al. specified that the attitude score was obtained by subtracting the total number of positive statements given one race from the total number of negative statements given the same race.   The range of scores for the pictures selected for each race was from +12 to -12. For each racial group only the score toward the other racial group was used.   The higher the positive score, the more favorable the attitude toward the other race.

Test Data

The authors developed the Projective Picture Test through repeated use with Negro and white children aged seven to thirteen.   Their investigation indicated that the test discriminated between the racial attitudes of Negro and white children.   A comparison of the mean of the white children in the three lower grades with the mean of the Negro children in the same grades revealed a significant difference (t = 3.50, .01 level).   Similarly, the means of Negro and white children of the fifth- and sixth-grades showed a significant difference (t = 7.50, .01 level).   Both differences were in the direction of more undesirable descriptions being assigned to Negro pictures by white children than by Negro children.

Radke et al. used the same photographs from the Projective Picture Test in a Picture Sociometric Test to determine friendship choices of Negro and white children.   The data from the Picture Sociometric Test were consistent with the data from the Projective Picture Test.

Since the photographs used by Radke et al. in the Projective Picture Test were unavailable, the steps taken by the authors in the selection of photographs were repeated in the present study. Except for using different photographs, the procedure and behavioral descriptions were the same as in the Radke et al. study.

The Projective Picture Test was used in the present study to include in the test battery a more disguised test that did not directly question subjects about their racial attitudes.

In the present study the Projective Picture Test was given twice at an interval of two weeks to the same pupils used for reliability testing. There was a reliability coefficient of +.87 with 48 fourth- and fifth-grade white pupils. With 23 fourth- and fifth-grade Negro pupils, there was a reliability coefficient of +.88.

HOW I FEEL ABOUT OTHERS

Everybody has different feelings about everybody else. We like some people a lot, some a little bit, and some not at all. If the teacher knows these feelings, she can plan things better.

1. Which 4 persons in this class do you personally like the most? Write the 4 names below, and write a few words telling why you feel that way.

PUPIL'S NAME	WHY DO YOU LIKE EACH ONE?
Like most	
Like next most	
Like third most	
Like fourth most	

2. Which 4 persons in this class do you personally like the least? Write the names below, and write a few words about what makes you feel that way about each one.

Like the least	
Like next least	
Like third least	
Like fourth least	

MY TEACHER

Pretend that you could have your teacher change in some way. Please mark the way you would like to have your teacher in this class act by checking the circle (0) on each line that best tells how you would like her to be.

	Much more than she does now	A little more than she does now	The same as she does now	A little less than she does now	Much less than she does now
1. Help with work	0	0	0	0	0
2. Make sure work is done	0	0	0	0	0
3. Make us work hard	0	0	0	0	0
4. Make us behave	0	0	0	0	0
5. Ask us to decide	0	0	0	0	0
6. Trust us on our own	0	0	0	0	0
7. Get angry	0	0	0	0	0
8. Act friendly	0	0	0	0	0
9. Show that she understands how we feel	0	0	0	0	0
10. Help us under- stand each other	0	0	0	0	0

170

CLASSROOM LIFE

Here is a list of some things that describe life in the classroom. Circle the number of the statement that best tells <u>how this class is for you</u>.

A. Life in this class with your regular teacher
    1. has all good things.
    2. has mostly good things.
    3. more good things than bad.
    4. has about as many good things as bad.
    5. more bad things than good.
    6. has mostly bad things.

B. When I'm in this class I
    1. usually feel wide awake and very interested.
    2. pretty interested, kind of bored part of the time.
    3. not very interested, bored quite a lot of the time.
    4. don't like it, feel bored and not with it.

C. The pupils in this class help one another with their schoolwork
    1. most of the time.
    2. sometimes.
    3. hardly ever.
    4. never.

D. The pupils in this class act friendly toward each other
    1. always.
    2. most of the time.
    3. sometimes.
    4. hardly ever.

E. The pupils in this class do what the teacher wants them to do
    1. most of them do.
    2. more than half do.
    3. less than half do.
    4. hardly anybody does.

F. If we help each other with our work in this class the teacher
    1. likes it a lot.
    2. likes it some.
    3. likes it a little.
    4. doesn't like it at all.

G.   How hard are you working these days on learning
      what is being taught in school?
      1. very hard.
      2. quite hard.
      3. not very hard.
      4. not hard at all.

HOW THIS CLASS THINKS

School classes are quite different from one another on how pupils think and feel about school work, about one another, and about teachers. How do you think this class (your classmates) feel about the following things? (Circle one of the numbers under How Many Think this Way?)

	HOW MANY THINK THIS WAY?				
	Almost everyone in the class thinks this	Many pupils in the class think this	About half in the class think this	Some pupils in this class think this	Only a few in the class think this
1. It is good to ask and answer many questions in classroom work	1	2	3	4	5
2. Asking the teacher for help is a good thing to do	1	2	3	4	5
3. It is good to help other pupils with their schoolwork (not including tests)	1	2	3	4	5
4. Schoolwork is more often fun than it is not	1	2	3	4	5
5. The teacher really understands how pupils feel	1	2	3	4	5
6. If you work very hard, others in this class will not like it	1	2	3	4	5
7. The teacher expects pupils to put too much time on schoolwork	1	2	3	4	5

173

MY TEACHER

Scoring

Each of the ten items of My Teacher was treated separately. The five possible responses for each item were grouped into three categories: those indicating teacher change in a greater direction (much more, a little more); the desire for the teacher to remain the same as now; and those indicating teacher change in a lesser direction (much less, a little less).

CLASSROOM LIFE

Scoring

The separate items of Classroom Life were treated as separate scores. For every item, the lower the score the more positive the view of classroom life. The score for each item was based on the number of available responses. Item A has six choices, with a consequent score of 1 to 6, depending on the response selected. Items B through G have four options, with a score of 1 to 4.

HOW THIS CLASS THINKS

Scoring

The seven items of How This Class Thinks were treated as separate scores. For items 1 through 5, the lower the score the more positive the view of classroom life. For items 6 and 7, the higher the score the more positive the view of classroom life. With each item having five choices, the item scores ranged from 1 to 5, depending on the option chosen.

TRIP RATING SHEET

1. How do you feel about the trip?

    _____ Liked it a lot

    _____ Liked it a little

    _____ In between

    _____ Did not like some of it

    _____ Did not like it at all

2. How much do you want to have the same partner for another trip?

    _____ Very much

    _____ A little

    _____ In between

    _____ Not much

    _____ Not at all

3. Who had better ideas?

    _____ My partner had much better ideas

    _____ My partner had a little better ideas

    _____ We both had good ideas

    _____ I had a little better ideas

    _____ I had much better ideas

Scoring

The three items of the Trip Rating Sheet were treated as separate scores. For all of the items, the lower the score the more positive the feeling toward the activity group program and the partner. Each item, with five possible responses, has a score of 1 to 3. For items one and two, a score of 1 indicates positive feeling, a score of 3 indicates negative feeling, and a score of 2 indicates an in-between feeling. For item three, a score of 1 indicates an equality with the partner, a score of 3 indicates that the subject values his own ideas more than his partner's, and a score of 2 indicates that the subject values his partner's ideas more than his own.

A total score for the three trips was calculated for each item. These scores were divided into four categories. The first category consisted of those subjects with a total score of 3 (all scores on items 1 and 2 consistently in the positive direction and on item 3 consistently equating partner's and subject's ideas). The second category contained those subjects with a total score of 9 (all scores on items 1 and 2 consistently in the negative direction and on item 3 consistently valuing subject's ideas more than his partner's). A third category consisted of those subjects with a total score of 6 (for items 1 and 2 all scores reflecting the in-between option and for item 3 all scores valuing partner's ideas more than own). The fourth category, unlike the other three, was composed of those subjects who were inconsistent in their choice of options, scoring 4, 5, 7, or 8.

TEACHER-DISCUSSION LEADER RATING SHEET

1. How good a job did your teacher do in helping
    make this a good trip?

    _____ Very good job

    _____ Good job

    _____ In between

    _____ Bad job

    _____ Very bad job

2. How good a job did the discussion leader do in
    making a good discussion?

    _____ Very good job

    _____ Good job

    _____ In between

    _____ Bad job

    _____ Very bad job

TEACHER-DISCUSSION LEADER RATING SHEET

Scoring

The two items of the Teacher-Discussion Leader Rating Sheet were treated as separate scores. For the items, the lower the score the more positive the feelings toward the teacher and the discussion leader. The five options of each item were scored similarly to the Trip Rating Sheet. The scores of 1 to 3 and the four categories of the total score have the same meaning as on items 1 and 2 of the Trip Rating Sheet.

ADMINISTRATION OF TESTS AND RATING SHEETS

Attitude Tests and Supplementary Tests

The tests were administered early in the school
term, before the start of the Activity Group Program,
in accordance with arrangements with the teachers of
all 16 classes. The tests were administered by an
adult with teaching experience.

In a brief orientation, the pupils were told that
the test administrator was engaged in research with
scientists at Columbia University that involved the
cooperation of pupils in responding to written statements. They were told that the results would in no
way affect their grades in the class, and that only
the scientists would see the results. Also, since
they were not so much tests as questionnaires, it
was suggested that there were no right or wrong
answers. The pupils were informed that the scientists
were interested in their opinions. No indication was
made of any relationship between the Activity Group
Program and the tests.

At the conclusion of the Activity Group Program
several months later, only the attitude tests were
administered again--in the same way, to the same
classes, and by the same administrator. No indication was made to indicate any relationship between
the Activity Group Program and the tests.

Rating Sheets

The Trip Rating Sheet was administered twice
during each trip, at the conclusion of the Trip
Activity and at the conclusion of the Discussion
Activity. The Teacher-Discussion Leader Rating Sheet
was administered once at the conclusion of the
Discussion Activity. All the tests were administered
by the discussion leader.

In a brief orientation, the pupils were told
that their opinions about the trip would be helpful
for improving future trips.

NOTES

1. B. Robert Tabachnick, "Some Correlates of Prejudice Toward Negroes in Elementary Age Children," Journal of Genetic Psychology, C (1962), 193-203.

2. William J. Goode and Paul K. Hatt, Methods in Social Research (New York: McGraw-Hill, 1952).

3. Donald T. Campbell, "Social Distance Scale," in Oscar K. Buros, ed., The Fourth Mental Measurements Yearbook. (Highland Park, N.J.: The Gryphon Press, 1953), pp. 88-89.

4. Goode and Hatt, loc. cit.

APPENDIX D

RESULTS OF INITIAL TESTING OF ATTITUDE MEASURES:
MEANS, STANDARD DEVIATIONS, SIGNIFICANCE TESTS
OF RACIAL DIFFERENCES, TREATMENT GROUP
DIFFERENCES, BOY-GIRL DIFFERENCES

TABLE 11

Means and Standard Deviations of Pre-Scores of the
Attitude Scale for Treatment Groups of Negro and
White Fourth-Grade Pupils

	Negro			White		
	N	$\overline{X}$	S.D.	N	$\overline{X}$	S.D.
J-J	19	11.90	4.27	21	7.52	4.01
J-S	16	11.62	4.38	13	8.23	5.12
S-J	17	9.29	3.22	16	4.44	4.52
S-S	14	7.71	3.50	12	9.17	4.55
Totals	66	10.27	4.16	62	7.19	4.71

TABLE 12

Means and Standard Deviations of Pre-Scores of the
Social Distance Scale for Treatment Groups of
Negro and White Fourth-Grade Pupils

	Negro			White		
	N	$\overline{X}$	S.D.	N	$\overline{X}$	S.D.
J-J	19	24.74	10.49	21	13.81	12.87
J-S	16	22.31	11.80	13	16.15	12.67
S-J	17	19.76	11.89	16	8.00	10.81
S-S	14	9.14	11.09	12	19.75	20.32
Totals	66	19.56	12.45	62	13.95	14.35

TABLE 13

Means and Standard Deviations of Pre-Scores of the
Projective Picture Test for Treatment Groups
of Negro and White Fourth-Grade Pupils

	Negro			White		
	N	$\overline{X}$	S.D.	N	$\overline{X}$	S.D.
J-J	19	1.90	3.11	21	-5.43	3.23
J-S	16	3.06	3.09	13	-3.46	4.82
S-J	17	- .18	4.11	16	-3.06	2.86
S-S	14	- .29	4.38	12	-2.92	3.78
Totals	66	1.18	3.85	62	-3.92	3.72

TABLE 14

Significance Tests of Racial Differences in
Pre-Test Scores of Fourth-Grade
Pupils*

	Attitude Scale	Social Distance Scale	Projective Picture Test
t	3.68	1.99	6.08
significance level	.01	.05	.01
Msw	17.88	162.18	19.69
df = 120	.05 level = 1.98		.01 level = 2.63

*Based on analysis of variance

TABLE 15

Scheffé's Multiple Comparisons Test of Pre-Scores for Fourth-Grade Negro Pupils on the Attitude Measures

Group Comparisons	Attitude Scale Absolute Difference in Means	Significance Level	Social Distance Scale Absolute Difference in Means	Significance Level	Projective Picture Test Absolute Difference in Means	Significance Level
J-J vs. J-S	.28	ns	2.43	ns	1.16	ns
J-J vs. S-J	2.61	ns	4.98	ns	2.08	ns
J-J vs. S-S	4.19	ns	15.60	ns	2.19	ns
J-S vs. S-J	2.33	ns	2.55	ns	3.24	ns
J-S vs. S-S	3.91	ns	13.17	ns	3.35	ns
S-J vs. S-S	1.58	ns	10.62	ns	.11	ns
Msw	17.88		162.18		19.69	

TABLE 16

Scheffé's Multiple Comparisons Test of Pre-Scores for Fourth-Grade White Pupils on the Attitude Measures

Group Comparisons	Attitude Scale Absolute Difference in Means	Significance Level	Social Distance Scale Absolute Difference in Means	Significance Level	Projective Picture Test Absolute Difference in Means	Significance Level
J-J vs. J-S	.71	ns	2.34	ns	1.97	ns
J-J vs. S-J	3.08	ns	5.81	ns	2.37	ns
J-J vs. S-S	1.65	ns	5.94	ns	2.51	ns
J-S vs. S-J	3.79	ns	8.15	ns	.40	ns
J-S vs. S-S	.94	ns	3.60	ns	.54	ns
S-J vs. S-S	4.73	ns	11.75	ns	.14	ns
Msw	17.88		162.18		19.69	

TABLE 17

Means, Standard Deviations, and Scheffé's Tests
of Differences Between Fourth-Grade Boys
and Girls on the Pre-Test of the
Attitude Scale

| | White | | Negro | |
	Boys	Girls	Boys	Girls
$\overline{X}$	6.97	7.48	9.00	10.95
SD	4.55	4.98	3.67	4.29
N	35	27	23	43

| | Boys vs. Girls | | White vs. Negro | |
	White	Negro	Boys	Girls
Difference	.51	1.95	2.03	3.47
Significance Level	ns	ns	ns	.05
Msw	19.51			

TABLE 18

Means, Standard Deviations, and Scheffé's Tests
of Differences Between Fourth-Grade Boys
and Girls on the Pre-Test of the
Social Distance Scale

	White		Negro	
	Boys	Girls	Boys	Girls
$\overline{X}$	14.09	13.78	18.70	20.02
SD	13.62	15.52	10.74	13.38
N	35	27	23	43

	Boys vs. Girls		White vs. Negro	
	White	Negro	Boys	Girls
Difference	.31	1.32	4.61	6.24
Significance Level	ns	ns	ns	ns
Msw	182.40			

TABLE 19

Means, Standard Deviations, and Scheffé's Tests
of Differences Between Fourth-Grade Boys
and Girls on the Pre-Test of the
Projective Picture Test

	White		Negro	
	Boys	Girls	Boys	Girls
$\overline{X}$	-3.60	-4.33	1.83	.84
SD	3.74	3.72	3.93	3.81
N	35	27	23	43

	Boys vs. Girls		White vs. Negro	
	White	Negro	Boys	Girls
Difference	.73	.99	5.43	5.17
Significance Level	ns	ns	.01	.01
Msw	14.38			

189

TABLE 20

Means and Standard Deviations of Pre-Scores of
the Attitude Scale for Treatment Groups
of Negro and White
Fifth-Grade Pupils

		Negro			White	
	N	$\overline{X}$	S.D.	N	$\overline{X}$	S.D.
J-J	18	9.61	4.34	21	8.48	3.75
J-S	16	12.00	4.46	14	9.29	4.05
S-J	9	13.67	3.94	13	9.15	3.72
S-S	12	9.00	3.02	12	7.67	4.96
Totals	55	10.84	4.34	60	8.65	4.02

TABLE 21

Means and Standard Deviations of Pre-Scores of
the Social Distance Scale for Treatment
Groups of Negro and White
Fifth-Grade Pupils

		Negro			White	
	N	$\overline{X}$	S.D.	N	$\overline{X}$	S.D.
J-J	18	22.17	15.65	21	8.45	7.55
J-S	16	29.19	9.14	14	15.86	13.70
S-J	9	28.44	15.80	13	20.31	13.03
S-S	12	21.25	13.23	12	10.67	13.65
Totals	55	25.04	13.64	60	13.20	12.33

190

TABLE 22

Means and Standard Deviations of Pre-Scores of
the Projective Picture Test for Treatment
Groups of Negro and White
Fifth-Grade Pupils

| | Negro | | | White | | |
	N	$\overline{X}$	S.D.	N	$\overline{X}$	S.D.
J-J	18	1.94	4.61	21	-6.38	3.19
J-S	16	.5	3.88	14	-3.71	5.03
S-J	9	1.33	5.48	13	-3.85	4.98
S-S	12	-1.25	4.16	12	-5.92	3.87
Totals	55	.73	4.50	60	-5.12	4.29

TABLE 23

Significance Tests of Racial Differences in
Pre-Test Scores of Fifth-Grade Pupils*

	Attitude Scale	Social Distance Scale	Projective Picture Test
t	3.08	4.72	6.71
significance level	.01	.01	.01
Msw	16.70	158.93	18.80
df = 107	.05 level = 1.98		.01 level = 2.63

*Based on analysis of variance.

191

TABLE 24

Scheffé's Multiple Comparisons Test of Pre-Scores for Fifth-
Grade Negro Pupils on the Attitude Measures

Group Comparisons	Attitude Scale Absolute Difference in Means	Signif- icance Level	Social Distance Scale Absolute Difference in Means	Signif- icance Level	Projective Picture Test Absolute Difference in Means	Signif- icance Level
J-J vs. J-S	2.39	ns	7.02	ns	1.44	ns
J-J vs. S-J	4.06	ns	6.27	ns	.61	ns
J-J vs. S-S	.61	ns	.92	ns	3.19	ns
J-S vs. S-J	1.67	ns	.75	ns	.83	ns
J-S vs. S-S	3.00	ns	7.94	ns	1.75	ns
S-J vs. S-S	4.67	ns	7.19	ns	2.58	ns
Msw	16.70		158.93		18.80	

192

TABLE 25

Scheffé's Multiple Comparisons Test of Pre-Scores for Fifth-Grade White Pupils on the Attitude Measures

Group Comparisons	Attitude Scale Absolute Difference in Means	Significance Level	Social Distance Scale Absolute Difference in Means	Significance Level	Projective Picture Test Absolute Difference in Means	Significance Level
J-J vs. J-S	.81	ns	7.38	ns	2.67	ns
J-J vs. S-J	.67	ns	11.83	ns	2.53	ns
J-J vs. S-S	.81	ns	2.19	ns	.46	ns
J-S vs. S-J	.14	ns	4.45	ns	.14	ns
J-S vs. S-S	1.62	ns	5.19	ns	2.21	ns
S-J vs. S-S	1.48	ns	9.64	ns	2.07	ns
Msw	16.70		158.93		18.80	

TABLE 26

Means, Standard Deviations, and Scheffé's Tests
of Differences Between Fifth-Grade Boys
and Girls on the Pre-Test of the
Attitude Scale

	White		Negro	
	Boys	Girls	Boys	Girls
$\overline{X}$	8.67	8.64	10.67	11.00
SD	4.29	3.85	4.50	4.86
N	27	33	27	28

	Boys vs. Girls		White vs. Negro	
	White	Negro	Boys	Girls
Difference	.03	.33	2.00	2.36
Significance Level	ns	ns	ns	ns
Msw	17.73			

TABLE 27

Means, Standard Deviations, and Scheffé's Tests
of Differences Between Fifth-Grade Boys
and Girls on the Pre-Test of the
Social Distance Scale

	White		Negro	
	Boys	Girls	Boys	Girls
$\overline{X}$	12.37	13.88	27.52	22.64
SD	13.00	11.91	12.99	14.05
N	27	33	27	28

	Boys vs. Girls		White vs. Negro	
	White	Negro	Boys	Girls
Difference	1.51	4.88	15.15	8.76
Significance Level	ns	ns	.01	ns
Msw	167.99			

TABLE 28

Means, Standard Deviations, and Scheffé's Tests
of Differences Between Fifth-Grade Boys
and Girls on the Pre-Test of the
Projective Picture Test

	White		Negro	
	Boys	Girls	Boys	Girls
$\overline{X}$	-5.74	-4.61	1.44	.036
SD	3.99	4.51	4.94	4.00
N	27	33	27	28

	Boys vs. Girls		White vs. Negro	
	White	Negro	Boys	Girls
Difference	1.13	1.05	7.18	4.97
Significance Level	ns	ns	.01	.01
Msw	19.21			

APPENDIX E

PRODUCT-MOMENT CORRELATION COEFFICIENTS

TABLE 29

Product-Moment Correlation Coefficients Between Pre-Test Scores of the
Attitude Measures and Reading Scores and Ages for Negro and
White Fourth- and Fifth-Grade Pupils

	Fourth Grade			Fifth Grade		
	Attitude Scale	Social Distance Scale	Projective Picture Test	Attitude Scale	Social Distance Scale	Projective Picture Test
Negro Work						
Knowledge	+.410**	+.334**	+.238	-.158	-.146	+.201
Reading	+.422**	+.320**	+.258*	-.022	+.128	+.206
Age	+.026	+.020	-.129	+.035	+.021	-.223
White Word						
Knowledge	+.128	+.007	-.160	-.127	-.090	-.076
Reading	-.001	-.088	-.247	+.088	+.039	+.022
Age	+.259*	+.205	+.035	+.148	+.130	+.003

*Significant at .05 level.

**Significant at .01 level.

TABLE 30

Intercorrelations of Pre-Scores of the Attitude Scale, the Social
Distance Scale, and the Projective Picture Test for
Fourth- and Fifth-Grade Negro and White Pupils

Variable	1	2	3
1. Attitude Scale	—	+.624*(4th) +.642*(5th)	+.447*(4th) +.345*(5th)
2. Social Distance Scale		—	+.376*(4th) +.485*(5th)
3. Projective Picture Test			—

*Significant at .01 level.

TABLE 31

Product-Moment Correlation Coefficients Between Change Scores of the
Attitude Measures and Reading Scores and Ages for Negro and
White Fourth- and Fifth-Grade Pupils

	Fourth Grade			Fifth Grade		
	Attitude Scale	Social Distance Scale	Projective Picture Test	Attitude Scale	Social Distance Scale	Projective Picture Test
Negro						
Word						
Knowledge	-.211	-.037	-.176	+449**	+.114	+.058
Reading	-.168	+.040	-.188	+.302*	+.047	+.031
Age	+.059	+.167	-.036	-.277*	-.127	+.377**
White						
Word						
Knowledge	+.135	+.048	+.233	-.001	+.100	-.075
Reading	+.248	+.072	+.303*	-.003	-.023	-.261*
Age	-.208	-.067	+.001	-.188	-.205	-.012

*Significant at .05 level.

**Significant at .01 level.

201

TABLE 32

Intercorrelations of Change Scores of the Attitude Scale, the Social
Distance Scale, and the Projective Picture Test for Fourth-
and Fifth-Grade Negro and White Pupils

Variable	1	2	3
1. Attitude Scale	–	+.030 (4th) +.545* (5th)	+.105 (4th) -.095 (5th)
2. Social Distance Scale		–	+.038 (4th) -.099 (5th)
3. Projective Picture Test			–

*Significant at .01 level.

APPENDIX F

MEANS AND STANDARD DEVIATIONS OF PRE-, POST-, AND
CHANGE SCORES OF THE ATTITUDE MEASURES

TABLE 33

Means and Standard Deviations of Pre-, Post-, and Change Scores
of the Attitude Scale for Treatment Groups of
Negro and White Fourth-Grade Pupils

Group		Negro			White		
		Pre	Post	Change	Pre	Post	Change
J-J	$\bar{X}$	11.90	10.00	-1.90	7.52	9.26	1.71
	S.D.	4.27	5.32	4.11	4.01	4.97	4.12
	N	19	19	19	21	21	21
J-S	$\bar{X}$	11.62	9.81	-1.81	8.23	7.92	-.31
	S.D.	4.38	4.56	4.58	5.12	5.12	5.01
	N	16	16	16	13	13	13
S-J	$\bar{X}$	9.29	8.71	-.59	4.44	4.12	-.31
	S.D.	3.22	3.20	4.15	4.52	3.32	5.56
	N	17	17	17	16	16	16
S-S	$\bar{X}$	7.71	7.93	.21	9.17	7.67	-1.50
	S.D.	3.50	2.90	3.70	4.55	3.17	3.29
	N	14	14	14	12	12	12
Totals	$\bar{X}$	10.27	9.18	-1.09	7.19	7.34	.14
	S.D.	4.16	4.19	4.15	4.71	4.67	4.64
	N	66	66	66	62	62	62

TABLE 34

Means and Standard Deviations of Pre-, Post-, and Change Scores of the Social Distance Scale for Treatment Groups of Negro and White Fourth-Grade Pupils

Group		Negro			White		
		Pre	Post	Change	Pre	Post	Change
J-J	$\bar{X}$	24.74	24.05	-.68	13.81	14.48	.67
	S.D.	10.49	11.49	8.51	12.87	13.99	8.87
	N	19	19	19	21	21	21
J-S	$\bar{X}$	22.31	19.69	-2.62	16.15	19.77	3.62
	S.D.	11.80	16.17	11.79	12.67	13.69	9.73
	N	16	16	16	13	13	13
S-J	$\bar{X}$	19.76	13.53	3.76	8.00	4.00	-4.00
	S.D.	11.89	13.98	17.86	10.81	6.84	9.80
	N	17	17	17	16	16	16
S-S	$\bar{X}$	9.14	7.64	-1.50	19.75	21.92	2.17
	S.D.	11.09	13.43	9.63	20.32	17.64	17.03
	N	14	14	14	12	12	12
Totals	$\bar{X}$	19.56	19.38	-.18	13.95	14.32	.37
	S.D.	12.45	14.89	12.46	14.35	14.64	11.33
	N	66	66	66	62	62	62

TABLE 35

Means and Standard Deviations of Pre-, Post-, and Change Scores
of the Projective Picture Test for Treatment Groups of
Negro and White Fourth-Grade Pupils

Group		Negro			White		
		Pre	Post	Change	Pre	Post	Change
J-J	$\bar{X}$	1.90	.68	-1.21	-5.43	-4.62	.81
	S.D.	3.11	2.93	1.90	3.23	4.44	2.98
	N	19	19	19	21	21	21
J-S	$\bar{X}$	3.06	1.06	-2.00	-3.46	-3.54	-.08
	S.D.	3.09	3.49	3.27	4.82	5.12	1.98
	N	16	16	16	13	13	13
S-J	$\bar{X}$	-.18	-.29	-.12	-3.06	-4.62	-1.56
	S.D.	4.11	5.26	5.63	2.86	3.91	3.72
	N	17	17	17	16	16	16
S-S	$\bar{X}$	-.29	-.21	-.07	-2.92	-4.58	-1.67
	S.D.	4.38	5.32	4.50	3.78	3.94	3.75
	N	14	14	14	12	12	12
Totals	$\bar{X}$	1.18	.33	-.85	-3.92	-4.39	-.47
	S.D.	3.85	4.24	4.00	3.72	4.29	3.29
	N	66	66	66	62	62	62

TABLE 36

Means and Standard Deviations of Pre-, Post-, and Change Scores
of the Attitude Scale for Treatment Groups of
Negro and White Fifth-Grade Pupils

Group		Negro			White		
		Pre	Post	Change	Pre	Post	Change
J-J	X̄	9.61	11.72	2.11	8.48	8.38	-.10
	S.D.	4.43	4.57	2.72	3.75	4.22	2.70
	N	18	18	18	21	21	21
J-S	X̄	12.00	8.81	-3.19	9.29	9.29	0
	S.D.	4.46	4.36	3.43	4.05	6.11	4.64
	N	16	16	16	14	14	14
S-J	X̄	13.67	10.89	-2.78	9.15	11.77	2.62
	S.D.	3.94	5.06	4.44	3.72	3.74	3.18
	N	9	9	9	13	13	13
S-S	X̄	9.00	8.75	-.25	7.67	6.83	-.83
	S.D.	3.02	3.77	2.09	4.96	4.97	2.79
	N	12	12	12	12	12	12
Totals	X̄	10.84	10.09	-.74	8.65	9.02	.37
	S.D.	4.34	4.52	3.83	4.02	4.95	3.50
	N	55	55	55	60	60	60

TABLE 37

Means and Standard Deviations of Pre-, Post-, and Change Scores of the Social Distance Scale for Treatment Groups of Negro and White Fifth-Grade Pupils

Group		Negro			White		
		Pre	Post	Change	Pre	Post	Change
J-J	X̄	22.17	22.56	.39	8.48	14.43	5.95
	S.D.	15.65	15.97	12.42	7.55	11.92	10.59
	N	18	18	18	21	21	21
J-S	X̄	29.19	21.19	-8.00	15.86	20.79	4.93
	S.D.	9.14	15.03	14.19	13.70	14.62	11.66
	N	16	16	16	14	14	14
S-J	X̄	28.44	22.56	-5.89	20.31	23.46	3.15
	S.D.	15.80	16.76	16.94	13.03	14.76	13.18
	N	9	9	9	13	13	13
S-S	X̄	21.25	27.00	5.75	10.67	11.67	1.00
	S.D.	13.23	13.76	11.07	13.65	16.57	6.00
	N	12	12	12	12	12	12
Totals	X̄	25.04	23.13	-1.91	13.20	17.32	4.12
	S.D.	13.64	15.10	14.16	12.33	14.54	10.66
	N	55	55	55	60	60	60

TABLE 38

Means and Standard Deviations of Pre-, Post-, and Change Scores
of the Projective Picture Test for Treatment Groups
of Negro and White Fifth-Grade Pupils

Group		Negro			White		
		Pre	Post	Change	Pre	Post	Change
J-J	$\bar{X}$	1.94	1.78	-.17	-6.38	-7.24	-.86
	S.D.	4.61	3.46	3.63	3.19	3.11	3.54
	N	18	18	18	21	21	21
J-S	$\bar{X}$	.50	.38	-.12	-3.71	-5.14	-1.43
	S.D.	3.88	4.69	3.48	5.03	5.43	4.60
	N	16	16	16	14	14	14
S-J	$\bar{X}$	1.33	2.11	.78	-3.85	-4.31	-.46
	S.D.	5.48	6.09	3.93	4.98	4.33	4.10
	N	9	9	9	13	13	13
S-S	$\bar{X}$	-1.25	-.42	.83	-5.92	-5.75	.17
	S.D.	4.16	3.40	3.59	3.87	3.82	2.21
	N	12	12	12	12	12	12
Totals	$\bar{X}$	.73	.94	.22	-5.12	-5.82	-.70
	S.D.	4.50	4.32	3.56	4.29	4.20	3.68
	N	55	55	55	60	60	60

APPENDIX G

SIGNIFICANCE TESTS OF RACIAL DIFFERENCES IN
CHANGE SCORES

TABLE 39

Significance Tests of Racial Differences in Change
Scores of Fourth-Grade Pupils*

	Attitude Scale	Social Distance Scale	Projective Picture Test
t	-1.17	-.41	.35
significance level	ns	ns	ns
Msw	19.14	141.99	13.19
df = 120	.05 level = 1.98		.01 level = 2.63

TABLE 40

Significance Tests of Racial Differences in Change
Scores of Fifth-Grade Pupils

	Attitude Scale	Social Distance Scale	Projective Picture Test
t	2.31	-3.10	1.38
significance level	.05	.01	ns
Msw	10.66	147.47	13.57
df - 107	.05 level = 1.98		.01 level = 2.63

*Based on analysis of variance.

APPENDIX H

RELATIONSHIPS BETWEEN ITEMS OF TRIP RATING SHEETS
I AND II AND ATTITUDE SCALE CHANGE SCORES

TABLE 41

Relationship Between Item 1 of Trip Rating Sheet I
and Attitude Scale Change Scores

		Attitude Scale Change											
		Fourth-Grade						Fifth-Grade					
		White			Negro			White			Negro		
Group	Perception of Trip	+	0	-	+	0	-	+	0	-	+	0	-
J-J	Like	12	0	4	7	6	6	7	2	5	11	3	2
	Neutral	2	1	1	0	0	0	0	1	4	1	0	1
	Dislike	0	0	1	0	0	0	1	1	0	0	0	0
J-S	Like	5	0	7	6	1	6	4	0	3	1	1	8
	Neutral	0	0	0	0	0	3	2	0	1	1	1	4
	Dislike	0	0	1	0	0	0	1	0	3	0	0	1
S-J	Like	8	1	7	8	1	6	8	2	2	2	2	5
	Neutral	0	0	0	0	0	2	0	0	1	0	0	0
	Dislike	0	0	0	0	0	0	0	0	0	0	0	0
S-S	Like	2	2	4	4	6	0	2	2	3	4	1	4
	Neutral	0	1	3	0	0	1	1	0	4	0	0	2
	Dislike	0	0	0	0	2	1	0	0	0	1	0	0
Totals	Like	27	3	22	25	14	18	21	6	13	18	7	19
	Neutral	2	2	4	0	0	6	3	1	10	1	1	7
	Dislike	0	0	2	2	2	1	2	1	3	1	0	1

TABLE 42

Relationship Between Item 1 of Trip Rating Sheet II
and Attitude Scale Change Scores

		Attitude Scale Change											
		Fourth-Grade						Fifth-Grade					
		White			Negro			White			Negro		
Group	Perception of Trip	+	0	-	+	0	-	+	0	-	+	0	-
J-J	Like	12	0	3	5	5	6	7	2	5	11	3	2
	Neutral	1	1	2	2	1	0	0	2	3	0	0	1
	Dislike	1	0	1	0	0	0	1	0	1	1	0	0
J-S	Like	5	0	7	6	1	9	4	0	3	1	1	9
	Neutral	0	0	1	0	0	0	1	0	2	0	0	4
	Dislike	0	0	0	0	0	0	2	0	2	0	1	0
S-J	Like	8	1	7	8	1	7	8	2	1	2	2	5
	Neutral	0	0	0	0	0	1	0	0	2	0	0	0
	Dislike	0	0	0	0	0	0	0	0	0	0	0	0
S-S	Like	2	1	7	4	5	0	2	2	3	4	1	4
	Neutral	0	2	0	0	1	1	1	0	4	0	0	2
	Dislike	0	0	0	0	2	1	0	0	0	1	0	0
Totals	Like	27	2	24	23	12	22	21	6	12	18	7	20
	Neutral	1	3	3	2	2	2	2	2	11	0	0	7
	Dislike	1	0	1	0	2	1	3	0	3	2	1	0

TABLE 43

Relationship Between Item 2 of Trip Rating Sheet I
and Attitude Scale Change Scores

		Attitude Scale Change											
		Fourth-Grade						Fifth-Grade					
		White			Negro			White			Negro		
Group	Perception of Partner	+	0	−	+	0	−	+	0	−	+	0	−
J−J	Want	11	1	2	7	6	5	8	1	3	10	2	2
	Neutral	3	0	2	0	0	1	0	3	1	1	0	0
	Not Want	0	0	2	0	0	0	0	0	5	1	1	1
J−S	Want	5	0	4	5	1	5	5	0	1	1	1	5
	Neutral	0	0	0	0	0	2	0	0	1	0	0	5
	Not Want	0	0	4	1	0	2	2	0	5	0	1	3
S−J	Want	7	0	6	8	1	5	8	1	2	2	0	0
	Neutral	0	1	0	0	0	3	0	1	0	0	2	1
	Not Want	1	0	1	0	0	0	0	0	1	0	0	4
S−S	Want	1	3	2	2	4	0	2	0	3	4	0	5
	Neutral	0	0	2	0	3	1	1	0	1	0	1	0
	Not Want	1	0	3	2	1	1	0	2	3	1	0	1
Totals	Want	24	1	14	22	12	15	23	2	9	17	3	12
	Neutral	3	1	4	0	3	7	1	4	3	1	3	6
	Not Want	2	0	10	3	1	3	2	2	14	2	2	9

TABLE 44

Relationship Between Item 2 of Trip Rating Sheet II
and Attitude Scale Change Scores

		Attitude Scale Change											
		Fourth-Grade						Fifth-Grade					
		White			Negro			White			Negro		
Group	Perception of Partner	+	0	-	+	0	-	+	0	-	+	0	-
J-J	Want	10	1	2	7	6	6	8	0	2	10	2	1
	Neutral	4	0	1	0	0	0	0	2	1	1	0	1
	Not Want	0	0	3	0	0	0	0	2	6	1	1	1
J-S	Want	5	0	5	2	0	4	5	0	2	0	1	6
	Neutral	0	0	1	0	0	3	1	0	2	1	0	1
	Not Want	0	0	2	4	1	2	1	0	3	0	1	6
S-J	Want	5	1	3	6	1	5	6	1	3	2	1	3
	Neutral	0	0	2	2	0	1	1	1	0	0	0	0
	Not Want	3	0	2	0	0	2	1	0	0	0	1	2
S-S	Want	1	3	3	3	7	0	2	1	3	4	0	4
	Neutral	0	0	1	0	0	1	0	0	0	0	1	1
	Not Want	1	0	3	1	1	1	1	1	4	1	0	1
Totals	Want	21	5	13	18	14	15	21	2	10	16	4	14
	Neutral	4	0	5	2	0	5	2	3	3	2	1	3
	Not Want	4	0	10	5	2	5	3	3	13	2	3	10

TABLE 45

Relationship Between Item 3 of Trip Rating Sheet I and Attitude Scale Change Scores

		Attitude Scale Change											
		Fourth-Grade						Fifth-Grade					
		White			Negro			White			Negro		
Group	Perception of Partner Status	+	0	-	+	0	-	+	0	-	+	0	-
J-J	Equal	13	0	3	7	6	6	8	2	2	12	3	3
	Unequal	1	1	3	0	0	0	0	2	7	0	0	0
J-S	Equal	4	0	5	6	1	5	6	0	3	1	0	5
	Unequal	1	0	3	0	0	4	1	0	4	0	2	8
S-J	Equal	8	1	5	8	0	2	8	1	1	2	1	0
	Unequal	0	0	2	0	1	6	0	1	2	0	1	5
S-S	Equal	1	3	2	2	7	0	2	0	4	3	1	5
	Unequal	1	0	5	2	1	2	1	2	3	2	0	1
Totals	Equal	26	4	15	23	14	13	24	3	10	18	5	13
	Unequal	3	1	13	2	2	12	2	5	16	2	3	14

TABLE 46

Relationship Between Item 3 of Trip Rating Sheet II and
Attitude Scale Change Scores

		Attitude Scale Change											
		Fourth-Grade						Fifth-Grade					
		White			Negro			White			Negro		
Group	Perception of Partner Status	+	0	-	+	0	-	+	0	-	+	0	-
J-J	Equal	13	0	4	7	6	6	8	2	2	12	3	2
	Unequal	1	1	2	0	0	0	0	2	7	0	0	1
J-S	Equal	4	0	4	4	1	6	6	0	2	1	1	7
	Unequal	1	0	4	2	0	3	1	0	5	0	1	6
S-J	Equal	7	1	4	7	0	1	8	1	2	1	2	3
	Unequal	1	0	3	1	1	7	0	1	1	1	0	2
S-S	Equal	1	3	2	3	4	0	2	1	5	4	1	4
	Unequal	1	0	5	1	4	2	1	1	2	1	0	2
Totals	Equal	25	4	14	21	11	13	24	4	11	18	7	16
	Unequal	4	1	14	4	5	12	2	4	15	2	1	11

BIBLIOGRAPHY

BIBLIOGRAPHY

Axline, Virginia M. "Play Therapy and Race Conflict in Young Children," Journal of Abnormal and Social Psychology, XLIII (1948), 300-10.

Bayton, James A. "The Racial Stereotypes of Negro College Students," Journal of Abnormal and Social Psychology, XXXVI (1941), 99-102.

Bayton, James A., Austin, Lettie J., and Burke, Kay R. "Negro Perception of Negro and White Personality Traits," Journal of Personality and Social Psychology, I (1965), 250-53.

Bogardus, Emory S. "Measuring Social Distance," Journal of Applied Sociology, IX (1925), 299-308.

_____. "Measurement of Personal-Group Relations," Sociometry, X (1947), 306-11.

Boynton, Paul L., and Mayo, George D. "A Comparison of Certain Attitudinal Responses of White and Negro High School Students," Journal of Negro Education, XI (1942), 487-94.

Campbell, Donald T. "Social Distance Scale." The Fourth Mental Measurements Yearbook. Edited by Oscar K. Buros. Highland Park, N.J.: The Gryphon Press, 1953.

Clark, Kenneth B., and Clark, Mamie P. "Emotional Factors in Racial Identification and Preference in Negro Children," Journal of Negro Education, XIX (1950), 341-50.

_____. "Racial Identification and Preference in Negro Children." Readings in Social Psychology. Edited by Eleanor E. Maccoby, Theodore M. Newcomb, and Eugene L. Hartley. New York: Henry Holt, 1958.

Coleman, James S., et al. "Equality of Educational
    Opportunity." Racial Isolation in the Public
    Schools, Vol. 2, Appendices. Edited by United
    States Commission on Civil Rights. Washington,
    D.C.: U.S. Government Printing Office, 1967.

Cook, Stuart W. "Desegregation: A Psychological
    Analysis," The American Psychologist, XII (1957),
    1-13.

Criswell, Joan H. "A Sociometric Study of Racial
    Cleavage in the Classroom," Archives of Psychol-
    ogy, LXIII (1939), 1-82.

Deutsch, Martin. "Dimensions of the School's Role
    in the Problems of Integration." Integrating
    the Urban School: Proceedings of the Conference
    on Integration in the New York City Public
    Schools. Edited by Gordon J. Klopf and Israel
    A. Laster. New York: Teachers College,
    Columbia University, 1963.

Deutsch, Morton, and Collins, Mary E. "The Effect of
    Public Policy in Housing Projects upon Inter-
    racial Attitudes." Readings in Social Psychol-
    ogy. Edited by Eleanor E. Maccoby, Theodore M.
    Newcomb, and Eugene L. Hartley. New York:
    Henry Holt, 1958.

Fischer, John H. "Innovation and Two Currents of
    Change," Phi Delta Kappan, XLVI (1964), 151.

_____. "The School Park." Racial Isolation in
    the Public Schools, Vol. 2, Appendices. Edited
    by United States Commission on Civil Rights.
    Washington, D.C.: U.S. Government Printing
    Office, 1967.

Goldberg, Miriam L. "Factors Affecting Educational
    Attainment in Depressed Urban Areas." Educa-
    tion in Depressed Areas. Edited by A. Harry
    Passow. New York: Teachers College, Columbia
    University, 1963.

Goode, William J., and Hatt, Paul K. Methods in
    Social Research. New York: McGraw-Hill, 1952.

Gough, Harrison G., et al. "Children's Ethnic Atti-
    tudes: I. Relationship to Certain Personality
    Factors," Child Development, XXI (1950), 83-91.

Horowitz, Eugene L. "Race Attitudes." Characteristics of the Negro. Edited by Otto Klineberg. New York: Harper and Brothers, 1944.

Horowitz, Eugene L., and Horowitz, Ruth E. "Development of Social Attitudes in Children," Sociometry, I (1938), 301-38.

Institute for Social Research, Inventory of Classroom Study Tools for Understanding and Improving Classroom Learning Processes. Ann Arbor: University of Michigan Press, 1962.

Jenkins, Gladys, Shacter, Helen S., and Bauer, William W. These Are Your Children. Chicago: Scott, Foresman, 1966.

Lasker, Bruno. Race Attitudes in Children. New York: Henry Holt, 1929.

Lombardi, Donald N. "Factors Affecting Change in Attitudes Toward Negroes Among High School Students," Journal of Negro Education, XXXII (1963), 129-36.

Mayo, George D., and Kinzer, John R. "A Comparison of the Racial Attitudes of White and Negro High School Students in 1940 and 1948," Journal of Psychology, XXIX (1950), 397-405.

Radke, Marian, and Sutherland, Jean. "Children's Concepts About Minority and Majority American Groups," Journal of Educational Psychology, XL (1949), 449-68.

Radke, Marian, Sutherland, Jean, and Rosenberg, Pearl. "Racial Attitudes of Children," Sociometry, XIII (1950), 154-71.

Radke, Marian and Trager, Helen G. "Children's Perceptions of the Social roles of Negroes and Whites," Journal of Psychology, XXIX (1950), 3-33.

Radke-Yarrow, Marian, Campbell, John D., and Yarrow, Leon F. "Interpersonal Dynamics in Racial Integration" Readings in Social Psychology. Edited by Eleanor E. Maccoby, Theodore M. Newcomb, and Eugene L. Hartley. New York: Henry Holt, 1958.

Stauffer, Samuel A., Star, Shirley A., and Williams, Robin M., Jr. The American Soldier: Adjustment During Army Life. "Studies in Social Psychology in World War II," Vol. I. Princeton: Princeton University Press, 1949.

Tabachnick, B. Robert. "Some Correlates of Prejudice Toward Negroes in Elementary Age Children," Journal of Genetic Psychology, C (1962), 193-203.

Thompson, Daniel C. "Our Wasted Potential." Integrating the Urban School: Proceedings of the Conference on Integration in the New York City Public Schools. Edited by Gordon J. Klopf and Israel A. Laster. New York: Teachers College, Columbia University, 1963.

Thompson, George. Child Psychology. Boston: Houghton Mifflin, 1962.

United States Commission on Civil Rights, ed. Civil Rights, U.S.A. Public Schools Southern States. Washington, D.C.: U.S. Government Printing Office, 1962.

Valien, Bonita. "Community in Chaos, Cairo, Illinois." Schools in Transition: Community Experience in Desegregation. Edited by Robin M. Williams, Jr., and Margaret W. Ryan. Chapel Hill: University of North Carolina Press, 1954.

Webster, Staten W. "The Influence of Interracial Contact on Social Acceptance in a Newly Integrated School," Journal of Educational Psychology, LII (1961), 292-96.

Whitmore, Paul G., Jr. "A Study of Desegregation: Attitude Change and Scale Validation." Unpublished Ph.D. dissertation, University of Tennessee, 1956.

Wilner, Daniel M., Walkley, Rosabelle P., and Cook, Stuart W. Human Relations in Interracial Housing, A Study of the Contact Hypothesis. Minneapolis: University of Minnesota Press, 1955.

ABOUT THE AUTHOR

Julius Trubowitz, Assistant Professor in the Education Department at Queens College of the City University of New York, has had wide experience working with children in the school system. He has been a teacher and psychologist on every school level from elementary school through college.

Professor Trubowitz has served as a human relations consultant with various organizations, including school systems, nurses' associations, and police-community relations units.

Dr. Trubowitz studied at the University of Michigan and the City College of New York and received his doctorate in social psychology from Teachers College, Columbia University.

DATE DUE

22 Mar

29 Jul

1 Nov 74

GAYLORD

PRINTED IN U.S.A.